JUNIOR SOCCER:
A SESSION-BY-SESSION APPROACH

Frank Rowe and Glyn Jones

The Falmer Press

UK   Falmer Press, 1 Gunpowder Square, London, EC4A 3DE
USA Falmer Press, Taylor & Francis Inc., 1900 Frost Road, Suite 101.
Bristol, PA 19007

First published in 1996

A catalogue record for this book is available from the British Library

Library of Congress Cataloging-in-Publication Data are available on request

ISBN 0 7507 0500 0 paper

Jacket design by Caroline Archer

Typeset in 10/11 pt Times Ten by
Graphicraft Typesetters Ltd., Hong Kong.

Printed in Great Britain by Graphicraft Hong Kong on paper which has a specified pH value on final paper manufacture of not less than 7.5 and is therefore 'acid free'.

9.95
T.130.4
UYJ V
(Row)

Books are to be returned on or before
the last date below

JUNIOR SOCCER:

A SESSION-BY-SESSION
APPROACH

0750705004

Many thanks to my fiancee Mandy Chamberlain
for her support and professional advice
throughout the project.
Frank

CONTENTS

ACKNOWLEDGMENTS

The authors and publishers would like to thank the staff and children of Plascrug School, Aberystwyth and Mizuno UK for their cooperation in producing this book.

PREFACE

This book has been written to help both soccer coaches and those who teach 7–11 year olds in school deliver progressive and educationally worthwhile soccer sessions. A great many books have been written about the skills and strategies of the game but rarely do they address the unique demands of the coach faced with less than ideal circumstances **or** the school physical education lesson. Too often material is presented in such a way that only an experienced soccer coach could piece together a progressive programme of development from it. Frequently, skills are presented not in the sequence in which they are learnt but under headings such as 'passing', 'shooting' and 'heading' with little reference to **how** or **when** they should be introduced. Furthermore, such an approach provides little support for the teacher/coach in how to structure either a session or series of sessions. The intention of the following chapters is to present a progressive scheme of soccer sessions that are suitable for 7–11 year olds (and which meet the National Curriculum requirements for games in physical education). It is envisaged that the schemes of work be adopted throughout a child's junior years or, if preferred, dipped into as and when required to supplement an existing programme.

In this Preface and opening chapter, the tenor of delivery is directed towards the junior school teacher, however, the session-by-session approach is equally applicable to coaches working with junior soccer players.

For the Teacher
Educational reforms have placed a seemingly never ending increase on the demands of the junior school teacher's all-round expertise. Physical education, games and within it soccer, form one small part of the overall knowledge and experience which a teacher must deliver at Key Stage 2.

For the Coach
The advent of 'mini' teams and leagues has attracted many enthusiastic

(if somewhat inexperienced) coaches into positions of leading junior soccer programmes, often with little (if any) support.

The authors have combined their many years of experience in playing, coaching and teaching soccer in the belief that nowadays the effective teacher/coach must learn from others' experience.

Overview of Chapters The introductory chapter places the book within the context in which junior soccer is taught. It opens with a vignette describing a weak junior soccer session and this leads on to a discussion of the various factors impacting the nature of soccer provision. These include the principles underpinning the delivery of junior soccer, the constraints of inadequate facilities and equipment, educational developments in the field of Physical Education and the National Curriculum.

Chapters 2, 3, 4 and 5 cover the four junior years in school (7–11) and adopt a similar format; a block of twelve progressive soccer sessions being presented in each. The particular demands made by each year group and how these relate to the children's learning are discussed at the beginning of chapters 2 (7–9 years) and 4 (9–11 years). The book concludes with chapter 6, which provides guidance on assessment and a check list of technical skills covered in the sessions.

Features of the Book The sessions tackle both **content** and **delivery** aspects. Consequently, each one, in addition to its soccer content, contains useful teaching tips on error diagnosis and correction, methods of differentiation, motivational strategies and organizational hints. Moreover, opportunities to embrace the three strands of planning, performing and evaluating (as prescribed by the National Curriculum for Physical Education) are present throughout the sessions and appropriate teaching strategies outlined.

The sessions adopt a prescriptive approach and this is done to make the material more accessible to the many inexperienced junior soccer teachers/coaches. However, for those with greater experience, there is still a wide body of information which, if not used to replace current practice, will certainly augment it.

The Authors' Philosophy A brief final word on the **authors' philosophy** on the over-riding aim of a worthwhile soccer session should help to put their approach in perspective. A soccer session should provide every child with opportunity to enjoy and be successful in some aspect of the session and should focus on teaching the child rather than soccer. Such an approach opens up the broader opportunities for learning and thereby increases each child's chance to succeed through, and in, soccer.

We hope that our approach will enrich your soccer sessions and help create a positive learning environment for you and the children.

1   INTRODUCTION

The session begins by separating the boys and girls. The latter are sent off to play netball leaving the boys to have a game of soccer. Two teams of eleven are then picked by the 'captains' (who are selected because they are the best players) and the game (session!) begins. A largely one-sided game ensues for the next 30 minutes. Little Johnny scores three hat-tricks; Tim saves a penalty; Kieran hurts his leg whilst tackling; and Edward doesn't kick the ball for the second week in succession (although he did take a foul throw-in!). The red team eventually wins by the record margin of 23 goals to 2 and the session is over.

Good Teaching/ Coaching Practice

The caricatured session depicted above serves to illustrate a few of the teaching/coaching principles neglected in a poor soccer session. The following guidelines present a checklist of **good teaching/coaching practice in the soccer session** and underpin the approach adopted throughout the sessions in the coming chapters.

- Every child should be given the opportunity to succeed and enjoy the session. Repeated failure and a consequent lack of enjoyment are guaranteed to put the child off soccer for life!
- Mixed sex teaching groups should be encouraged. For 7–11 year olds there are no good reasons why boys and girls should not learn alongside one another.
- Each session should begin with a warm-up designed to prepare the body and mind for action.
- Stretches (although not included in the text for reasons of brevity) should proceed the warm-up and prepare the muscle groups to be used during the session.
- Each session should contain some skills learning, whether this be in the techniques and/or strategies of the game.
- Small-sided games (for instance 5 ∨ 5) should be adopted in preference to adult full-sized games.

1

- Teams and groups should be picked by the teacher/coach.
- Sessions should be progressive *ie*. each session builds on the previous one and skills learnt in a logical sequence.
- The rules and etiquette of the game should be taught during the session at appropriate moments.
- The safety of the children must be foremost in a contact sport. Consequently, fair play, the wearing of shinpads, good tackling technique, matching children for strength, size and so on must be addressed.

Developments in National Curriculum Physical Education

The National Curriculum has placed increasing emphasis on 'games' (including soccer) as an area of activity at Key Stage 2. In so doing, it is intended that not only skill levels in the game will improve but also that personal and social skills are developed. Consequently, the intended learning outcomes of soccer sessions embrace both personal and physical development goals and competencies such as good teamwork, perseverance and sportsmanship should be nurtured alongside the skills of the game.

There are a number of ways in which the National Curriculum requirements for physical education and games may be applied to a programme of soccer sessions and these are presented below:

1 Small-sided games should be employed *eg*. with a class of thirty children, three $5 \vee 5$ games are appropriate.
2 Basic tactics and strategies of the game should be taught – these should focus on attack and defence.
3 The core skills of soccer *ie*. sending (passing), receiving (controlling) and travelling (running with, or dribbling, the ball) should be covered.
4 Each session should have sufficient activity in it to promote health benefits in the child (approximately 20 minutes of sustained activity).
5 Basic physiological principles (such as the need to stretch adequately during a warm-up) should be introduced.

Although several foci are mentioned here, it is stressed that the principle concern of a soccer session should be educating the child through practising and performing the skills of the game.

Football in Context

Somewhat erroneously, a series of indifferent international performances by the home nations in both European and World Cup qualifying games, which highlighted inadequacies in skill levels of domestic players, were blamed partly on soccer teaching in schools. Although it might appear absurd to apportion blame on junior school teachers for the lack of skills displayed by international soccer players this conviction has, and will have, an impact on how soccer is taught.

Thus far, the **areas identified for improving the standards of soccer** throughout the nation centre upon the following principles:

(i)   The use of small-sided games.
(ii) An emphasis on individual skills learning.

(iii) The avoidance of too many competitive games (particularly where fundamental skills remain undeveloped).

However, such an approach, whilst promoting the development of skills in the game, does make increased demands on resources. Ideally, in the early stages of learning, the players should have a ball each. This allows them the time to develop their skills individually without the interruptions of having to share equipment. It is appreciated though that in under-resourced schools/clubs this is unlikely to happen and so a number of **strategies for delivering soccer sessions and dealing with inadequate facilities** and equipment are listed below:

- Whenever possible soccer sessions should be held outside.
- The nature of the playing surface will determine the suitability of various activities. For instance, concrete playgrounds are good for personal skills learning but less suitable for contact aspects of the game such as tackling. Conversely, playing fields are better suited to the rough and tumble elements of the game such as some goal-keeping skills, diving headers and tackling.
- If the amount of space is severely restricted then a number of steps may be appropriate. For instance, the use of skills circuits which alternate skills and fitness drills; the use of relay-type activities and the modification of equipment (for instance using foam or tennis balls).
- On occasions when it proves impossible to go outside, one of the sessions indicated with an asterisk should be selected (these take into account the demands of working within a confined space). **Note:** these sessions may be readily located using the tables in Chapter 6.
- Adequate equipment is essential to deliver a programme of soccer sessions. The sessions assume an average class/group size of thirty and that there is a minimum of one ball between two *ie.* fifteen balls per class/group (if this is not the case then additional balls must be purchased if the school/club is serious about delivering worthwhile sessions). As stop gaps, children may be able to bring in their own soccer balls or it may be possible to borrow some from a neighbouring school or club. *Note:* inadequate equipment (*eg.* one ball per class of thirty) makes offering a worthwhile soccer programme impossible.
- Pitch markings are not essential, although a gridded area (10×10m squares are ideal) is a useful teaching/coaching aid.
- Marker cones and bibs or braids also facilitate class/group organization and recognition of teams.
- If resources are inadequate for a class/group of thirty, but satisfactory for half the class, then it may be worth considering doing two activities simultaneously. For instance, whilst half the class are taught soccer the other half participate in a fitness circuit, they then change over activities half way through the session.

The Structure of the Sessions

Before moving on to the soccer schemes of work for each age group, it is important to draw the reader's attention to the framework which underpins the sessions and the principles adhered to which ensure continuity and progression within and between years.

Although the precise format occasionally does, and should, vary from one session to the next it is desirable to employ a similar working structure throughout a series of sessions. The majority of sessions presented in the coming chapters can be broken down in the following way:

Breakdown of a 45 Minute Soccer Session	
Warm-up	– 5 minutes
Skills warm-up/reinforcement	– 5 minutes
Skill development	– 15 minutes
Conditioned game	– 20 minutes

A variety of considerations determine the selection of appropriate material for each of the age groups. Between the age of 7 and 11 years, maturational changes in the child's development (and learning capabilities) render various teaching/coaching approaches less or more effective and are represented on the continuum below:

age 7	age 11
learning (individual) skills.	applying (team) skills.
learn attacking skills.	learn defensive skills.
work in small groups.	work in larger groups.
limited opposition.	increased opposition.
limited rules (and understanding of).	more complex games structure and rules.

However, other teaching/coaching strategies remain constant throughout the junior years and underpin all of the sessions presented.

1 The use of unequal sides (*eg.* 3 ∨ 1, 5 ∨ 2) to promote skills learning especially when teaching attacking skills, since equal sides tend to create a 'stalemate' situation if introduced too early.
2 Appropriate differentiation of material so that each child performs at their optimum level.
3 Adopting a variety of teaching styles to establish different learning environments.
4 To progress practices from a co-operative to competitive situation as skills improve – the aim of which is to 'groove' (make habitual) skills, thereby minimising their deterioration as the excitement of competition is experienced.

Guidelines for Delivering and Interpreting the Sessions

- Each session is presented in such a way that the information is readily accessible and may be used as an *aide-memoire* by the practising teacher/coach during a session.
- Precise interpretation of the text may not always be possible (*eg.* group sizes or the equipment available will vary) and so teachers/coaches should be prepared to make minor adaptations to some practices.

- When demonstrating a practice, highlight how it should **start** and **finish** and also, reinforce the **aim/purpose** of the practice.
- During the practices, try to establish the key factors causing a child to fail. Does the practice or technique (or both) require modification?
- A greater variety of warm-ups, skill practices and conditioned games is presented throughout the sessions than may be required – particularly as a certain amount of repetition facilitates learning. However, this has been done purposely so that activities which are compatible with the facilities, resources and ability of the children at individual schools/clubs may be adopted and those less appropriate dropped.
- The dimensions given for the various activities are merely guidelines and should be tailored to individual circumstances. For instance, a 5 ∨ 5 game would, ideally, be played on a 60 × 40m pitch. However, for three games to occur simultaneously the pitch sizes may need to be reduced. Compromise pitch sizes are indicated in the text and may require further refinement. In general terms, the more space in which the children have to play and practice the better.

Key to Diagrams

Bold letters *eg.* **A, B, C**	=	Players
x	=	Markers/cones
-------▶	=	Path of player
──────▶	=	Path of ball
◀—**10m**▶	=	Distance between markers/players in metres

Summary

Clearly, it is impossible to predict or encompass all of the many factors impinging on every junior soccer programme and individual schools/clubs may have to make minor alterations to the schemes of work outlined in the next chapters to suit their particular circumstances. Nevertheless, the general thrust and content of the sessions should not be beyond the capabilities of even the most modestly resourced school/club and where teacher/coach expertise is lacking, the prescriptive nature of the sessions is designed to promote confidence. Progressing through the schemes of work will develop soccer experience and expertise in the teacher/coach and we would encourage adaptations in their content as confidence and competence increase. Indeed, we would welcome any ideas you have for teaching soccer so that they might be included in future editions of the book. Please send your ideas to us at the following address: Frank Rowe and Glyn Jones; Department of Physical Education, Sports Centre, University of Wales, Aberystwyth, Dyfed, SY23 3DE.

PART I TEACHING SOCCER TO 7–9 YEAR OLDS

Introduction

The emphasis for 7–9 year olds is very much on activity and **enjoyment** with ample opportunity to touch the ball and improve skills. At this age, children do not work well in larger groups and co-operation is a skill which needs to be nurtured and developed gradually, building from pair work into small groups of three or four.

Players' concentration span is limited and so practices need to be varied and interspersed with mini-competitive games to maintain interest. However, it is important in a child's early encounters with the game to develop confidence and competitive situations which provide **every** child with the opportunity to succeed should be employed.

The basic technical aspects of the game (passing, control, unopposed heading, shooting and goalkeeping) and a very rudimentary understanding of team strategy should be introduced. Players should be encouraged to play in all positions (including goalkeeping) so that they have the opportunity to learn all the skills of the game. Whilst players are still learning the basic skills, the introduction of defenders should be limited and their role may initially be a passive one.

Quality repetition of the core skills is essential to ensure that they do not deteriorate in the competitive situation. To facilitate this, good technique should be reinforced whilst technical errors in performance need to be identified and eradicated as soon as possible.

Because the majority of the practices will be new to the children, it is important to invest time reinforcing good working routines which will be adopted throughout the soccer programme. For instance, by employing easily recalled names which identify specific practices (or games) *eg.* the 'pass and follow' practice, you will greatly improve the speed at which the class can be organised into similar practices in subsequent sessions.

Games should be relatively straightforward to understand and complex rules avoided. Thus enabling the games to 'flow' uninterrupted by disputes over obscure technicalities (*eg.* the off-side law). Such an environment is promoted if children begin to take on the responsibility of officiating their own games (whilst playing) without having to constantly refer to the teacher/coach for adjudication. This is particularly important when there are three games continuing simultaneously.

Remember – The essential requirement is that **you and the children enjoy the soccer sessions** and that a feeling of success (whether it be in the planning, performing or evaluating of the game) is engendered in each individual.

2 TWELVE SOCCER COACHING SESSIONS: 7–8 YEARS

7–8 YEARS: SESSION 1

- **Intended learning outcome:** Introduce players to the 'push pass' (used for short, accurate passing) emphasising the 'monkey' position and striking the ball with the inside of the foot.

- **Equipment:** Ball between two, marker cones.

	Content/Organisation	*Teaching Points*
• **Warm-up**	1 Running around the pitch/ playground. On command 'one' – touch ground, 'two' – jump in air and 'three' change direction.	1 Encourage quick responses to the commands. As confidence increases give combinations of commands *eg.* 'one, three, two' etc. . . .
• **Skills Warm-up/ Reinforcement**	1 Developing warm-up, run in any direction dodging one another. Respond to commands 'stop' and 'turn' (from running forwards to backwards or vice versa)	1 **Safety:** encourage good all-round awareness rather than speed to avoid collisions and don't allow running backwards for further than a few metres.
• **Skill Development**	1 Introduce the 'push pass'.	1 Inside of kicking foot contacts middle of ball. Body position slightly crouched (in monkey position) with non-kicking foot alongside ball.
	2 If you are not confident/ competent to perform it, 'shadow' the movement (*ie.* move through it without performing it)	
• **Skill Practice 1**	1 Players are in pairs, facing each other 3–4m apart. Position markers 2m apart to form passing channels and pass back and forth.	1 To **differentiate** the task passers may stand closer or further apart, or channels narrowed/widened.

Skill Practice 1 diagram:

```
    A     B     C
    ↑     ↑     ↑
x   |  x  |  x  |  x
    ↓     ↓     ↓
    D     E     F
```

Error diagnosis: the passing leg should be slightly flexed, not rigid, and follow through to the target not 'stab' at the ball.

If necessary, players may use their hands to help stop/ control the ball.

Plate 1: Pupils practice 'push' pass in passing channels spaced 2m apart.

	Content/Organisation	Teaching Points
• **Skills Practice 2**	1 Organisation as above. How many passes can they make in 30 seconds? 2 Rotate partners and repeat – can they beat their previous score?	1 Ask players what makes a good pass?' **Accuracy and weight**.
• **Conditioned Game**	**'Beat the Clock'** Teams of 5 ∨ 5. **Team A** stands in a circle and makes as many passes as possible in the time it takes **Team B** to run, in relay, around them. **A** and **B** change over, the team with the highest total of passes wins.	As teams become more proficient, passes may be made around the 'clock' rather than randomly across it and after each pass the time called out *ie*. 1 'o'clock, 2 'o'clock etc. . . . The distance between players (*ie*. the size of the clock) may be increased or decreased as appropriate.

Team A

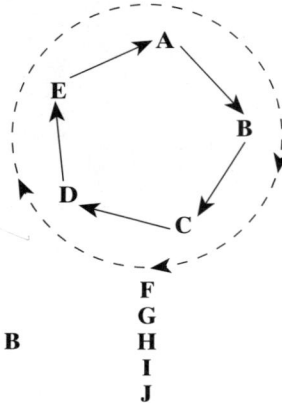

Team B

	F
	G
	H
	I
	J

• **Conclude Session**

Reinforce the intended
learning outcomes with 3
quick questions.

1 What is the name of the pass
we looked at today?
Push pass

2 Which part of the foot kicks
the ball in the 'push pass'?
Inside

3 What is the correct body
position for the pass?
Monkey

7–8 YEARS: SESSION 2

- **Intended learning outcome:** Introduce players to controlling/receiving the ball with the foot, emphasising the importance of relaxing the controlling area on impact.

- **Equipment:** Ball between two, marker cones, beanbags or skittles.

	Content/Organisation	*Teaching Points*
• **Warm-up**	See previous session.	
• **Skills Warm-up/ Reinforcement**	1 As for Skill Practice 1.	1 After a short practice, time passes made by pairs in 30 seconds.
	2 Develop above so that a target (beanbag or skittle) is placed in the passing channel, which players then attempt to hit.	2 **Race** – first pair to hit the target 3 times.
• **Skill Development**	1 Introduce control with the foot.	1 Use all parts of the foot (top, bottom, inside and outside) to take the pace off (control) the ball so that it can then be passed.
	2 Have a player roll a ball into yourself (or another player) to demonstrate technique.	2 Foot should be relaxed so that the ball is controlled just in front of the player.
• **Skill Practice 3**	1 As before, using passing channels, with emphasis now on control.	1 Encourage as few touches as possible before passing the ball back. Players may need to hand feed the pass if push pass is not accurate enough.
• **Skill Practice 4**	1 Using the passing channels, the receiver now stands 1m back from the 2 markers. The server stands 3m back and feeds the ball (underhand) to the receiver who aims to control the ball without it bouncing back between the cones.	1 Progress to feeding with the push pass. Get players to change roles frequently. Aerial or bounce feed may be appropriate for more able. **Error diagnosis:** foot may be moving at ball on control causing it to bounce away –

13

Content/Organisation   *Teaching Points*

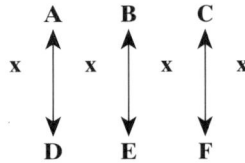

emphasise 'cushioning' the
ball.

• **Conditioned Game**

'Ticking Bomb'
Teams of 6. **Team A** stand
in a circle with one team
member in the middle. This
player passes and receives
the ball, in turn, from each
player around the circle.
Meanwhile, **Teams B, C** and
D are doing likewise. First
team to pass around the
circle jump in air shouting
'BOOM'.

Try to match ability of
middle players.

Practice is easily adapted to
compete against the clock *ie.*
How many passes can each
middle player make in 30
seconds?

Allow each team member to
have a turn in the middle.

• **Conclude Session**

Reinforce intended learning
outcomes.

1 What do we call the skill we
looked at today?
Control

2 Which part of the foot do we
use for control?
All parts

3 How do we control the ball?
Relax and cushion

14

7–8 YEARS: SESSION 3

- **Intended learning outcome:** Introduce players to travelling with the ball (dribbling) emphasising the importance of 'pushing' the ball with relaxed feet.

- **Equipment:** Ball between two, marker cones.

	Content/Organisation	*Teaching Points*
• **Warm-up**	1 Run around dodging one another. Call number and players must get into groups of that size. 2 On number 2, pairs have to go between each others legs.	1 Numbers up to 5 work best. Emphasise getting into correctly sized groups as quickly as possible.
• **Skills Warm-up/ Reinforcement**	1 Ball per pair in 20m grid. Moving within grid push passing with partner.	1 Encourage pair to stay within 3m of each other. Avoid other pairs.
• **Skill Development**	1 Introduce basics of dribbling.	1 Keep ball close to feet. Use all parts of the foot, relax foot and push ball.
• **Skill Practice 5**	1 Using 20m grid and ball per pair (**A** and **B**). **A**s dribble in grid whilst **B**s jog around the outside. Call out a body part (*eg.* left foot, right knee) which **A**s must stop ball with. **B**s then change over with **A**s.	1 Players with ball try and avoid each other. Encourage **B**s to remain alert and to change over quickly with **A**s.
• **Skill Practice 6**	1 As above, only **B**s spread out in grid and stand still with legs apart. **A**s dribble ball between as many different **B**s legs as possible in 60 seconds. Change over.	1 Encourage players to spread out to avoid bottle necks. Having dribbled through one player's legs must move on to another player.
• **Conditioned Game**	'**Dribbles**' Teams of 4 ∨ 4. **Team A** stand in a 10m square. How many passes can they make around it in 1 minute? Whilst **Team B** (split in 2 × 2 facing each other 5m apart) count	Players to call out score as game progresses. Who do they think will win, the dribbles or the passes?

Content/Organisation	*Teaching Points*
how many times they can dribble between two markers placed between them. **B** dribbles to **C**, **C** to **A** and so on.	Distances between players in teams may be altered to ensure a close match.

Team A

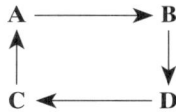

Team B

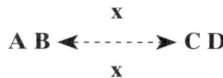

• **Conclude Session**	Reinforce intended learning outcomes.	1 Should the ball remain close to the feet when dribbling? **Yes**
		2 Why do you think this is important? **Retain possession and can pass/shoot**

Plate 2: Dribbling within a 20m square. The group shows good close control, although they need to work on getting their heads up!

7–8 YEARS: SESSION 4

- **Intended learning outcome:** Consolidate and develop learning from sessions 1–3.

- **Equipment:** Ball between two, marker cones.

	Content/Organisation	Teaching Points
• **Warm-up**	See previous session.	
• **Skills Warm-up**	1 In groups of five, players form a circle. 'Pass and follow' ball to anyone in the circle.	1 To make a circle, get the players to hold hands in a circle, let go, and then take three steps back. Have players call out the name of the person to whom they are passing. **Note:** it helps if players think of a name before they have to pass!
• **Skill Development**	Reinforce learning of push pass, foot control and dribbling from sessions 1–3.	Whilst players are performing skills, periodically stop them and ask about the techniques.
• **Skill Practice 7**	Two simultaneous activities.	Two activities allows one group to have a ball each.
	1 Half players are put into groups of 4. Each group is split 2 × 2 facing each other 5m apart.	1 First, allow players to run through the practice without a ball. Introduce ball when familiar with where to run. Call out '**pass and follow**' to remind them. How many passes can they make in 30 seconds?

C A ⟷ B D

◀── 5m ──▶

A push passes to **B** and runs to back of opposite queue. **B** controls ball, push passes to **C** and runs to back of opposite queue etc. . . . .

2 In 20m grid set up a number of 'gates' (markers 2m apart).

2 Allow time to practise skills before seeing how many

17

Players have a ball each and dribble it through as many different gates as possible.

gates they can pass through in 30 seconds.

This practice may be adapted so that players have to navigate a course whilst dribbling. How long does it take them?

3 Change over the groups.

- **Conditioned Game**

'No Man's Land'
In groups of seven, the aim is for two teams of 3 to pass the ball safely through 'no man's land' which is defended by one player (**D**). If the ball is intercepted then the defender changes place with the passer.

Note: rules may need modifying to ensure the same player isn't always defending.

To help get the practice started allow the first pass across no man's land to be free (*ie.* it can't be intercepted).

Teams are allowed up to 3 passes in the end zones to create an opening before passing to the other end zone.

Each time the ball successfully crosses no man's land a goal is scored.

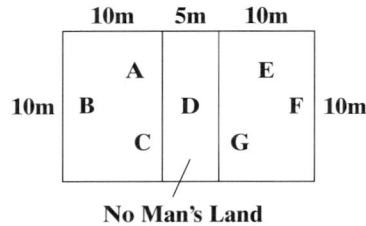

```
        10m    5m    10m
       ┌─────┬─────┬─────┐
       │  A  │     │  E  │
  10m  │B    │  D  │    F│ 10m
       │  C  │     │  G  │
       └─────┴──/──┴─────┘
```

No Man's Land

- **Conclude Session**

Reinforce intended learning outcomes from sessions 1–4.

7–8 YEARS: SESSION 5

- **Intended learning outcome:** Introduce players to the basic skills of heading, emphasising use of the forehead and keeping eyes open.

- **Equipment:** Ball between two, marker cones, braids.

	Content/Organisation	Teaching Points
• **Warm-up**	1 In pairs (**A** and **B**), jog around 20m square. On whistle, **A** tries to get away from **B** in the square. On second whistle, **A** and **B** stop. How far has **A** got from **B**? Repeat several times.	1 Encourage a quick stop. Look for good dodging skills and changes in direction. Alternate role of **A** and **B**.
• **Skills Warm-up/ Reinforcement**	1 In groups of four, players 'pass and move' within a 10m square.	1 Encourage sideways and backwards runs after pass. When passing, call name of intended receiver.
• **Skill Development**	1 Introduce basic heading skills. If you don't want to head yourself, demonstrate correct technique by having player lob (underarm throw with high trajectory) ball to you and catch it in front of forehead.	1 Keep eyes open and contact ball on forehead. Head meets ball not vice-versa. **Safety:** do not use heavy balls to head with or allow too many headers whilst technique is poor.
• **Skill Practice 8**	1 In pairs (2–3m apart), feeder lobs ball to partner to head back. Increase/decrease the distance between pairs as appropriate. Emphasise the importance of a good **two-handed** feed/lob.	1 Allow three attempts and change over – repeat. **Error diagnosis:** ball contact is on top of head/bridge of nose – catch ball in front of forehead and self-feed.
• **Skill Practice 9**	1 In 3's, 5m apart. **A** feeds **B** who directs header towards **C**. Five feeds per player – who can direct the most headers to the catcher?	1 **Error diagnosis:** inaccurate headers may be as a result of closed eyes or failure to direct forehead towards target on impact.

Content/Organisation

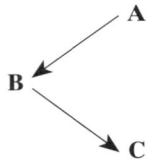

Teaching Points

Differentiate practice by altering the distance/angle between players. **Note**: it is easier to head the ball back in the direction from which it was fed.

Plate 3: Notice the eyes fixed on the ball and a good body position for this header.

• **Conditioned Game**	**Small-sided Game** Games of 4 ∨ 4, small goals (2m apart) on 30 × 20m pitch. No goalkeepers, let the players decide on rules for restarts. Rotate teams so that they play different opposition after 5 minutes. Pitches should be organised thus:	A number of games will be occurring simultaneously, thus it is important that players learn to 'referee' their own games (*ie.* agree on and abide by their own rules). Pick teams which are equally matched and use the braids to differentiate teams.

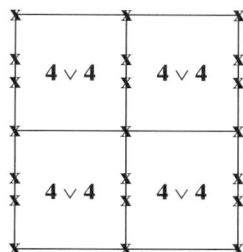

• **Conclude Session**	Reinforce intended learning outcomes.	1 Which part of the head should be used for heading? **Forehead** 2 What else is it important to do whilst heading? **Keep eyes open**

7–8 YEARS: SESSION 6*

- **Intended learning outcome:** Introduce players to a four station skills circuit, reinforcing and developing skills covered in sessions 1–5.

- **Equipment:** Ball between two, marker cones, braids, 2 benches, skittles, bean bags, ropes.

	Content/Organisation	*Teaching Points*
• **Warm-up**	See previous session.	
• **Skills Warm-up/ Reinforcement**	1 In groups of four, players stand in a cross formation with a skittle/marker in the centre.	1 Distance between pairs will depend on space available (ideally 3m). **Differentiate** activity by increasing/decreasing passing distance or size of target. For able players, bring in 'two-touch' restriction (*ie.* one touch to control and one to pass).

```
        A
        ↑
C ←─── x ───→ D
        ↓
        B
```

One ball per pair, **A** and **B** pass back and forth attempting to hit skittle (as do **C** and **D**) – which pair can register three hits first?

• **Skill Development**	1 Introduce the skill circuit *ie.* demonstrate the four activities comprising the circuit. Divide class into four groups and assign each one to an activity.	1 Make one clear point for each activity (too much information will only be forgotten). On the first rotation around the activities make sure everyone knows where they are going **before** they set off.
• **Skill Practice 10**	**A Skills Circuit.** **Activity 1**: *Passing* – two benches are laid out on floor 10m apart facing each other. Players pass against one bench, control ball turn and dribble towards other bench and repeat.	1 A wall may be used instead of benches. If too congested, players to work in pairs and take turns after set number of passes. Emphasise – foot through middle of ball to keep it on the ground.

Content/Organisation	*Teaching Points*
Activity 2: *Heading* – In pairs, **A** lob feeds to partner **B** who heads ball back and then performs 3 star jumps. Repeat 5x and change over.	2 This is a fitness as well as heading practice. More able players may jump and head.
Activity 3: *Dribbling* – Set up a course using markers, beanbags, ropes, cones etc. . . . Players to dribble around it without touching obstacles.	3 To avoid congestion, have players begin course at different starting points.
Activity 4: Two teams of 4 ∨ 4 in grid. Team in possession of ball attempts to make 5 throw and catches without defending team intercepting — if successful, score a goal. If ball is intercepted (or goes out of grid) possession changes over. Introduce restriction of no passes over head height.	4 This is a good practice for introducing the concept of getting into space (*ie.* spreading out) when team is in possession of ball. It is also good for practising goalkeeping skills of catching and throwing.

• **Conclude Session**

Reinforce learning from **Activity 4**.

When your team gains possession, what should the team members do? **Spread out**

7–8 YEARS: SESSION 7

- **Intended learning outcome:** Introduce basic skills of goalkeeping, emphasising the correct stance and pulling the ball into the chest when catching.

- **Equipment:** Ball between two, marker cones, braids.

	Content/Organisation	Teaching Points
• **Warm-up**	1 Players run around a figure of eight circuit.	1 Jog around the circuit first before introducing various running forms.

	Content/Organisation	Teaching Points
	Along each straight a different form of running is employed. a – jog normally b – side skips c – knees up running d – backwards running	Ensure players are well spaced out (they don't all have to be on the same straight) Intersperse activity with stretches and phase in new activities one at a time to include: e – sprints f – heel to bottom running g – skipping h – hopping
• **Skills Warm-up/ Reinforcement**	1 In 4's, players stand at four corners of 10m grid. **A** dribbles to **B**, **B** to **C**, **C** to **D** etc.... **Note:** after players have dribbled they should run backwards to the corner they dribbled from. Place markers along sides which must be dribbled around.	1 Encourage close control (*ie.* keeping ball close to feet) and use of both feet. Player to stop ball at end of dribble by placing foot on top of ball.
	2 Progress to races between teams – which team is first to get all players back to their original starting place?	2 Expect skill levels to deteriorate in the competitive situation.
• **Skill Development**	1 Introduce the basic stance for goalkeeping. Similar to monkey position in Session 1, therefore reinforce this and introduce one new teaching point at a time.	1 Stance is such that goalkeeper can react quickly. Body position is slightly crouched, feet shoulder width apart, eyes on ball, hands just above waist height, fingers spread and palms towards ball.

Content/Organisation	Teaching Points

	2 Catching the ball and pulling it into the chest. Why is ball pulled in? **Stop attackers from getting it**	2 Ball is caught with both hands and pulled in quickly to the chest. Emphasise importance of getting body behind ball when catching.
• **Skill Practice 11**	1 In pairs (using passing channels in Skill Practice 1), **A** rolls ball (by hand) to **B** who saves and returns for **A** to save – repeat.	1 Initially feed should be directly to the keeper. As proficiency increases, ball may be fed to either side of keeper who should then move to get body behind ball.
	2 Progress so that **A** push passes for **B** to save. **B** rolls ball back, **A** controls and push passes back etc. . . . After 5 saves, **A** and **B** change over roles.	2 At this stage feed should remain on ground. Pace of feed will depend on keeper's ability.
• **Skill Practice 12**	1 In pairs, **A** is seated with legs astride, straight and in front. **B** hand feeds ball to either side of **A** who catches and gathers ball to chest whilst rolling to side.	1 Feeding player should stand close enough to deliver an accurate feed. **Safety:** pull arms in and roll over shoulder.
• **Conditioned Game**	'**Fetball**' Teams of 5 v 5, play in 20m square. Two benches are placed at opposite ends of square. **Team A**'s keeper stands on one bench and **B**'s the other. Played like netball in open play, goals are scored by heading the ball to your own teams keeper. The ball must not be kicked and netball rules apply for gaining/retaining possession.	Reinforce use of space when in attack (Session 6). Regularly alternate keepers so that everyone has a turn. If heading is poor, then ball may be thrown to keeper for one goal and headed for two goals. Use braids to differentiate teams. **Safety**: heading should be unopposed.
• **Conclude Session**	Reinforce intended learning outcomes.	1 Who can show me the keepers stance? 2 Why is it important to be in this position? **Helps to react quickly** 3 What should we do when catching the ball? **Position body behind ball and pull it into chest**

7–8 YEARS: SESSION 8*

- **Intended learning outcome:** Develop passing and control skills, emphasising the need for movement after passing.

- **Equipment:** Ball between two, marker cones, braids.

	Content/Organisation	Teaching Points
• Warm-up	See previous session.	
• Skills Warm-up/ Reinforcement	1 Groups of six stand in a circle passing a ball to each other. After each pass, run backwards 5m and then forwards 5m back to circle. 2 As above, only after each pass run around circle to where ball was passed. 3 As above, only 'pass and follow' as in Session 4.	1 Moving backwards after a pass is an important skill to learn, especially when an attacking team is trying to create space. 2 This is a tiring practice and should only continue in short bursts.
• Skill Development	1 Introduce the importance of moving off (without) the ball, in order to create space and passing options for the player on (with) the ball.	1 Because these activities are tiring, stop players more frequently, drawing attention to good quality work. Whilst learning the practices, it is helpful to have players 'walk through' them before attempting to jog or run.
• Skill Practice 13	1 In 3's, **A** passes to **B** and follows pass to a mid-point 'x' before running backwards to starting position. **B** passes to **C** and runs to mid-point and back etc. . . . . To encourage accurate passing, place 2m goals at mid-points of triangle sides (which serve as targets to pass through).	1 If player passes strongly with one foot encourage them to try using their weaker foot. Because the ball is coming in from one direction and leaving in another, make sure players turn to face in the direction they are passing.

Content/Organisation	Teaching Points

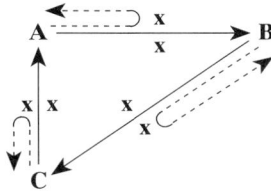

2 Change direction of passing around triangle.	2 Progress practice by introducing competition. How many passes in 30 seconds?

- **Skill Practice 14**

1 In 6's, players pass and run **backwards** to the back of their line.	1 Players should be aware of what is behind and in front of them (occasionally glance over shoulder) when running backwards.

	Develop into competition as above.

- **Conditioned Game**

'Crab Football' Teams of 6 v 6, aim is to score goals as in football only players are in the crab position *ie.* with hands on the ground. Goalkeepers are allowed to kneel (on a mat to protect knees) and use their hands to protect 3m wide goal.	If indoor space is large enough, run 2 games at once. If not, rotate teams into game frequently (every 3–4 minutes). Do not wait for goals to be scored before changing teams over.

- **Conclude Session**

Reinforce intended learning outcomes.	Why is it important to move after giving a pass? **To support/help the player on the ball** **To create space for the player (or team) on the ball**

7–8 YEARS: SESSION 9

- **Intended learning outcome:** Introduce players to shooting, emphasising use of the instep (strike ball along boot laces, with toes pointing downwards).

- **Equipment:** Ball between two, marker cones, braids.

	Content/Organisation	Teaching Points
• **Warm-up**	**'The Bean Game'** Players perform a series of different activities in response to different beans which you call out *eg*. 'runner' – run on spot 'jumping' – jump on spot 'broad' – star jumps 'chilli' – shake 'butter' – melt to ground 'baked' – lie down (in sun)	Introduce one bean at a time and, as players become more competent at responding, speed up the change from one bean (activity) to the next. Intersperse activity with stretches.

- **Skills Warm-up/ Reinforcement**

1 In 4's (2 × 2) 5m apart, 'pass and follow' (see Skills Practice 7i).

2 As above only pairs stand diagonally opposite.

AB
CD

3 **AB** and **CD** continue practice as above. **GH** and **EF** perform same pass and follow practice diagonally across **AB** and **CD**.

AB   GH
EF   CD

Teaching Points:

1 Encourage as few touches as possible before passing the ball back.

2 Players should learn to control and pass with the ball coming and going from a variety of angles (as in the game).

Note: players to face straight forward.

3 This practice is more complex and will require a clear demonstration. Have players walk through the practice until familiar with it.

It introduces players to passing and moving in a more congested area.

Passes and runners should attempt to avoid one another and this will require good awareness.

	Content/Organisation	*Teaching Points*
• Skill Development	1 Introduce basics of shooting. **Note:** it is useful to have something to stop shots *eg.* a goal with nets, a wall or appropriate fencing. If none are available, players should take turns to retrieve shots.	1 The basics for good shooting technique are: to use the instep, knee of striking leg over ball (*ie.* do not lean back – or shot goes too high), non-striking foot alongside ball with head down and still.

• Skill Practice 15

1 **A** rolls ball (by hand) to player **B** who shoots from 8m between 2 markers 5m apart. C retrieves/saves ball and returns it to **A**. Change roles after five shots.

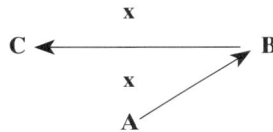

```
              x
    C  ◄───────────────►  B
              x
              A
```

Safety: organise so that players shoot away from a central area and not towards others who are practising. Use goals if available.

2 Which group of 3 can score the most goals in 30 seconds?

1 Encourage controlled low shots (no more than 1m above ground) rather than all out power.

Error diagnosis: common faults include striking ball with toes (emphasise kick with laces) and ball going too high and/or slicing (emphasise knee over ball). Also keep head still whilst shooting.

2 This practice encourages accuracy.

• Conditioned Game

Teams of 5 ∨ 5 (plus 2 keepers) play on 40 × 30m pitch. Each team nominates 4 attackers and 1 defender. Attackers are only allowed in attacking half of pitch and defenders in the defending half. Thus, excluding the keeper, there is a 4 ∨ 1 situation in either half of the pitch weighted in favour of the attack.

Attackers should be encouraged to utilise their additional players by spreading out.

Players should shoot when they get the opportunity.

It is important to alternate solitary defender and keepers frequently (*ie.* every 2 minutes).

Uneven sides helps promote attacking skills.

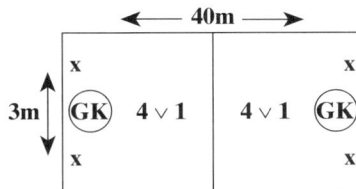

```
            ◄──── 40m ────►
        ┌───────────┬───────────┐
        │ x         │         x │
   3m ↕ │ (GK)  4∨1 │ 4∨1  (GK) │
        │ x         │         x │
        └───────────┴───────────┘
```

	Content/Organisation	*Teaching Points*
	Defender is allowed to play ball out of own half unopposed.	
• **Conclude Session**	Reinforce intended learning outcomes.	1 Which part of the foot should kick the ball for the shot we practised today? **Instep (along laces)**
		2 Why do we want to keep the shot low? **More difficult to save and won't go over goal**

7–8 YEARS: SESSION 10

- **Intended learning outcome:** Introduce players to opposition, emphasising the importance of relaxing (which will facilitate good control) and providing support for the player with the ball.

- **Equipment:** Ball between two, marker cones, braids.

	Content/Organisation	Teaching Points
• **Warm-up**	See previous session.	
• **Skills Warm-up/ Reinforcement**	1 In pairs, **A** rolls/passes ball alternately to two markers (5m apart) placed on either side of **B**. **B** controls ball and passes back to **A**. Repeat 10 times and change over.	1 For practice to be effective, **A**'s feed must be accurate. Therefore may need to roll with hands.

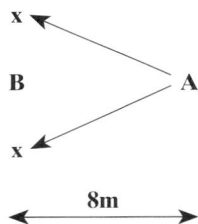

8m

At first, **A** should let **B** reach each marker before passing.

As confidence/competence increases, **A** should pass to the opposite marker from which **B** is. This is a more complex skill for both **A** and **B**. **A** has to pass into space (requiring good weight of pass) and **B** is moving whilst controlling the ball.

• **Skill Development**	1 Introducing an opponent to passing and control practices. Important: Introduce the following activities using throwing and catching skills.	1 This will tend to increase errors. Stress the need to relax and concentrate on the skill (whether it be control or passing) rather than the opponent.
• **Skill Practice 16**	1 In 5's, four attackers along sides of 10m square with defender (**E**) in middle.	1 Encourage attackers to move in support of the player with the ball.

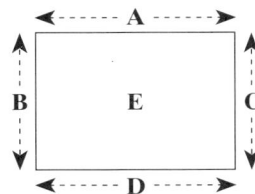

Attackers can move along their side of square (but

If defender intercepts pass then changes places with attacker who made pass.

If attackers make 5 successful passes score a goal and change the defender.

Do not allow the same player to defend for too long.

nowhere else). They inter-pass with one another whilst defender **E** (who is not allowed out of square) tries to intercept.

• **Skill Practice 17**

1 As above, but 3 attackers and 1 defender. Attackers are allowed to move to an adjacent side if no other player is there.

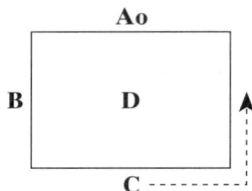

```
         Ao
    ┌──────────┐
  B │    D     │ ↑
    └──────────┘┊
         C ┄┄┄┄┄┄┘
```

1 After a practical demonstration, ask players which side they think is the worst side on which to stand to help the player with the ball?
The one directly behind the defender.

In diagram, **C** moves to support the player with the ball (**Ao**).

• **Conditioned Game**

'Keep Ball'
In 5's, four attackers versus one defender in 20m square. Attackers have to make 5 passes without defender touching ball to score. If defender intercepts pass, changes roles with attacker. If ball leaves square, player responsible becomes defender. After goal is scored, last attacker to touch ball becomes defender.

The ratio between defenders and attackers may be varied depending on players' ability.

Encourage attackers to spread out and position themselves so as to help the player with the ball.

For this game to work well, the defender should be encouraged to chase after the ball. Change defenders regularly and give them lots of praise.

• **Conclude Session**

Reinforce intended learning outcomes.

1 How can you help the player with the ball?
Move to a position where they can pass to you

2 What should the player with the ball do as an opponent approaches?
Relax and concentrate on performing the skill

7–8 YEARS: SESSION 11

- **Intended learning outcome:** Reinforce and develop learning covered in sessions 7–9, employing a four station skills circuit.

- **Equipment:** Ball between two, marker cones, braids.

	Content/Organisation	Teaching Points
• **Warm-up**	**'Tag Ball'** Nominate 6 players as taggers to hold a ball in their hands. They chase after rest of class and tag by placing (not throwing) the ball against them. Tagged player then becomes tagger and takes the ball.	Before commencing, have players jog around area designated for tag game. Intersperse activity with stretches.
• **Skills Warm-up/ Reinforcement**	1 In 6's, 5 attackers circle one defender. Attackers attempt to pass ball without defender intercepting. If ball leaves circle, attacker responsible changes with defender or if defender intercepts pass changes with attacker. 5 successful passes scores a goal and then change the defender.	1 Reinforce importance of good control through relaxing and concentrating. Circle should be 7–8m in diameter. First pass is 'free' (*ie*. it musn't be intercepted). To simplify, this practice can be introduced as a catching and throwing activity (no throws above head height).
• **Skill Development**	1 Introduce the skill circuit *ie*. demonstrate the 4 activities and divide class equally around them. A work card detailing/ demonstrating the activity will help explain and remind what is expected.	1 Make one clear point for each activity. On the first rotation around activities, make sure everyone knows where they are going **before** they set off and what they will be doing next.
• **Skill Practice 18**	**Activity 1**: *Heading* – In 3's with 2 balls, A x ◄---- C ----► x B	1 Feeders should allow **C** to stop at marker before feeding ball for header (*ie*. **C** performs a stationary header)

33

Content/Organisation	Teaching Points
C runs to marker in front of **A**. **A** feeds ball for **C** to head back. **C** runs to marker in front of **B**. **B** feeds and **C** heads back. Repeat for 8 headers and change over roles.	Stress use of forehead (not top of head) for header and eyes open for as long as possible. **A** and **B** should be 15m apart. **C** heads it 1–3m depending on ability.
Activity 2: '*Ball Skills*' – ball per pair. **A** performs a skill with the ball (using hands, feet or head), can **B** repeat it?	2 Players to experiment within 10m grid and demonstrate different ideas to the group/class.
Activity 3: *Goalkeeping* – ball per pair. **Keeper A** attempts to throw the ball into the goal of **keeper B**. **B** attempts to save/prevent **A** from scoring. **B** then attempts to score past **A**. Goals should be approximately 10m apart and 3m wide.	3 Practice develops throwing and saving skills. Emphasise importance of getting body behind shot (throw) if possible. Vary distance between goals (and goal size) depending on power of throw and space available. Throws should not go above head height. **Safety:** if indoors, mats on ground allow keeper to dive.

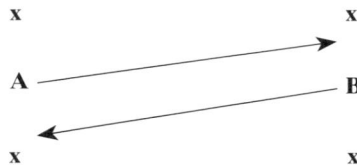

x   x

A ————————————→ B

x   x

Content/Organisation	Teaching Points
Activity 4: In 5's (4 ∨ 1). Four attackers attempt to stop ball in 2m square area at centre of 25m square playing area. Defender tries to stop them and is not allowed in 2m square.	Play restarts from any corner of the ouside square if a goal is scored, the defender gains possession, or the ball leaves the playing area. Encourage attackers to spread out (making defence difficult). Change defender frequently.

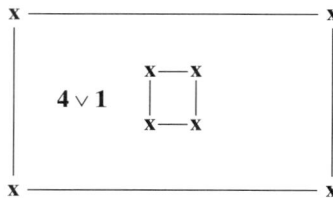

x ————————————— x

4 ∨ 1   x — x

x ————————————— x

Content/Organisation	Teaching Points
• **Conclude Session**	
Reinforce intended learning outcomes.	1 Why do you think it is important for the goalkeeper to get their body behind a shot?

Content/Organisation	*Teaching Points*
	If fails to catch it, body will stop ball entering goal
	2 Which part of the head is used for heading? **Forehead**
	3 Why do you think it is important to spread out in activity 4? **So defender can't mark everybody**

7–8 YEARS: SESSION 12

- **Intended learning outcome:** Introduce players to a mini 5-a-side tournament.

- **Equipment:** 12 balls, goal posts (or marker cones), braids.

	Content/Organisation	*Teaching Points*
• **Warm-up**	**'Tunnel Relay'** Organise players into 6 teams of 5 (which they will remain in for the tournament). First member of each team (**A**) dribbles ball round marker (20m away) and back. Rest of team stand in a line and pass another ball alternately over head and between legs until **A** returns. Team then stands with legs apart (forming a tunnel) which **A** passes ball down. Back player stops ball and repeats role of **A**. **A** joins front of line.	Relay is complete when last player to dribble passes ball down tunnel and team sits quietly in line. Demonstrate relay with a practical run through and allow a practice run before the race begins. Try to balance teams for ability.
• **Skills Warm-up/ Reinforcement**	1 Teams of five stand in circle. Players throw to anyone in the circle and follow ball. As above, only push pass and control (rather than throw and catch) skills used.	1 Encourage accurate throws/ passing and as few touches to control as possible. How many passes can they make in thirty seconds?
• **Skill Development**	Introduce players to tournament format.	Every team will get 3 games. Team scoring most goals in those games wins.
• **Skill Practice 19**	**Mini 5-a-side Tournament** Divide 6 teams into two pools of 3. Each pool will play round robin (all teams play each other) on that pool's pitch (*ie.* 2 pitches will be in operation).	Matches should be played concurrently so that only 2 teams are not participating at any given time. Non-participating teams should help retrieve balls, stretch and/or (depending on space) practice their skills. For the last three games of the tournament create a third

Content/Organisation	*Teaching Points*
Pool 1 **Pool 2** A ∨ B D ∨ E B ∨ C E ∨ F C ∨ A F ∨ D	pitch (if space allows) so all can be played at once.

Each match to last 5 minutes and number of goals scored by each team recorded. Highest goal scorers from Pool 1 play their counterparts in Pool 2. Runners up play each other as do the teams scoring least in each pool.

Teams should rotate their goalkeeper.

Note: if only space for one pitch, shorten the duration of games (3 minutes) and provide an activity for non-participating teams which can be performed in small area set aside *eg.* skipping, mini-fitness circuit, hopscotch etc. . . .

Try and say something positive to every player during the tournament.

• **Conclude session**

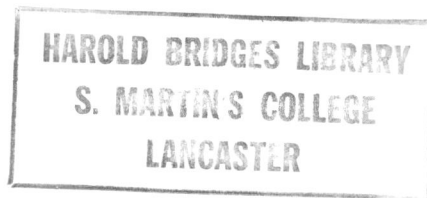

Emphasise the good points that came out in the tournament. A good pass, save or goal. A team that spread out well when in possession and so on.

This is the conclusion to a year's work – congratulate the children for all their hard work so that they look forward to next year's soccer programme.

For your notes

3 TWELVE SOCCER COACHING SESSIONS: 8–9 YEARS

8–9 YEARS: SESSION 1

- **Intended learning outcome:** Develop the skills of the 'push pass' and control, focusing on receiving the ball from one direction and passing it in another and the importance of the 'first touch'.

- **Equipment:** Ball between two, marker cones, braids.

	Content/Organisation	*Teaching Points*
• **Warm-up**	**'Stuck in the Football Mud'** A tag game, 4 braided taggers are nominated and players they tag stand still with legs apart, circling their arms. 4 other players (dribblers) have a ball each and only they can free a tagged player by passing ball between their legs. The freed player then takes the ball to free somebody else. **Note:** players with ball cannot be tagged.	Arms should brush past ears on circling. Frequently change the taggers over with the dribblers. Game can be introduced by having 'dribblers' carry ball and roll it through legs. This game may be introduced through playing 'stuck in the mud' (*ie.* without dribblers).
• **Skills Warm-up/ Reinforcement**	1 As for Skill Practice 1 and 2, (pages: 10–11) 2 Develop practice so that after each pass players touch ground with both hands.	1 Encourage 'two-touch' football *ie.* one touch to control and one to pass. 2 Whilst touching the ground on either side of feet, players should keep eyes on ball.
• **Skill Development**	Introduce skill of receiving the ball from one direction and passing it in another.	**Emphasise:** importance of the 'first touch' (the control) to create the angle for the pass. **Note:** for more able players, controlling ball with outside of foot opens up new angles for pass.
• **Skill Practice 20**	1 In 3's, **A** push passes ball 5m to **B** through 2 markers. **B** controls ball and passes ball to **C** through 2 markers. **C** then passes to **B** etc. . . .	1 **Progressions:** a) **B** controls ball, turns with ball and passes to **C**. b) **B** controls ball to side, turns and passes. c) **B** controls ball to side whilst turning and passes

A

x | x

B ← → C

x

x

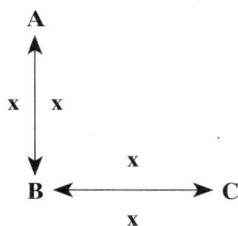

Change over roles after 6 passes by **B**.

to **C**. (This is an advanced skill which only the most able will be able to perform)

• **Skill Practice 21**

1 In 4's, players stand at corners of 10m square. Pass ball around outside of square (first to left and then right).

2 First team to pass ball around square three times?

3 Pass and follow around square and jog backwards to starting position.

1 Make sure players look at target before passing.

Encourage good quality passing (weight and accuracy).

2 Or/and, how many passes in thirty seconds and compare with scores for (3). Which practice do players think they will score higher in?

3 How many passes in thirty seconds?

• **Conditioned Game**

'Chase Ball'
In 5's, organisation as for Skill Practice 21(i) only additional player has to chase the ball around the square. Can they catch it up?

Everyone to have a turn at chasing.

Differentiate game by:

(i) allowing one pass head start before chase begins.

(ii) shortening/lengthening sides of square.

(iii) allowing players to throw and catch as well/ instead.

• **Conclude Session**

Reinforce intended learning outcomes.

1 What is the important skill we looked at today?
First touch or control

2 Why do you think this skill is so important?
Because it enables a player to do the next skill with the ball (today, it was change direction of pass)

8–9 YEARS: SESSION 2

- **Intended learning outcome:** Develop control skills, emphasising use of the thigh as a controlling area and the need to 'cushion' the ball.

- **Equipment:** Ball between two, marker cones, braids.

	Content/Organisation	Teaching Points
• Warm-up	See previous session.	
• Skills Warm-up/ Reinforcement	1 In pairs inside 20m square, players move and pass whilst avoiding others.	1 Encourage short passes and changes in direction.
	2 As above only players may inter-pass with anyone. For both practices encourage players to spread out.	2 It is important that players call out name of intended recipient of pass.
• Skill Development	1 Introduce control on the thigh.	1 The thigh is raised until almost horizontal to the ground to receive the ball. On impact the thigh 'cushions' (ie. withdraws) so that the ball drops gently in front of the player. Arms should be held out slightly to aid balance.
	2 Have a player lob the ball to you to demonstrate technique (note: if not confident/ competent to perform skill, use progression b outlined below to demonstrate it).	
• Skill Practice 22	1 In pairs using passing channels, **A** lob feeds ball to **B** to control on thigh and push pass back. Change over after 5 attempts. **Error diagnosis:** thigh 'thrusts' at ball causing it to bounce away. Emphasise cushioning ball (as if ball was landing on a feather bed).	1 **Progressions:** a) player self-feeds, catches ball with thigh and hands together, drops ball whilst withdrawing thigh and passes to partner to do same. b) As above only partner feeds ball.

Ball leaves thigh too high/
low – alter angle of thigh
on impact as appropriate.

c) As for (b) only controls
on thigh without using
hands to help.

Plate 4: A progression for control on the thigh is to catch the ball on the controlling area
and then, withdrawing the thigh, allow the ball to drop to the ground.

	Content/Organisation	*Teaching Points*

• Skill Practice 23

1 Teams of 4 ∨ 4 on 20 × 15m pitch with 2m end zones.

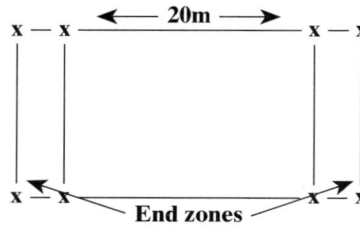

```
x — x  ◄—— 20m ——►  x — x
   |                    |
   |                    |
   |                    |
x ◄—x                 x —► x
      └─ End zones ─┘
```

Teams play throw and catch netball rules but score by controlling ball on thigh and stopping it dead in their opponents end zone.

1 No over-head passing.

No defenders are allowed in the end zones.

Encourage use of space and movement after pass.

If fail to control/stop ball in the End zone – defending team gains possession.

• Conditioned Game

As for Skill Practice 23 only football rules apply and goals are scored by stopping the ball in opponent's end zone.

Players to decide their own rules for restarts (*ie.* when a goal has been scored or the ball goes out of play).

Game may be modified by nominating 2 players (one from each side) as 'floaters'. Floaters wear distinguishing bibs and are always on the side of the team in possession. Thus attackers always have a 5 ∨ 3 advantage.

• Conclude Session

Reinforce intended learning outcomes.

1 What do I mean when I say 'cushioning'?
Taking the pace off/stopping the ball

2 How is this achieved?
Withdraw the controlling surface on impact

8–9 YEARS: SESSION 3

- **Intended learning outcome:** Develop dribbling skills, emphasising awareness of the ball and playing situation.

- **Equipment:** One ball between two, marker cones.

	Content/Organisation	*Teaching Points*
• Warm-up	As for 'Stuck in the Football Mud' (page: 40) only replace 'dribblers' with 'headers'. They free tagged players by heading ball to them (self-feed) to catch – they then become a 'header'.	Headers should not attempt to head the ball too far (1–2m is far enough).
• Skills Warm-up/ Reinforcement	1 Ball between 2, 10m apart. **A** dribbles ball around partner, returns to starting position and passes ball to **B** who repeats.	1 Encourage quality of dribbling (*ie.* keeping ball close to feet) before speed. Organise players in rows so that pairs do not run across one another.
• Skill Development	1 Introduce Skills Practice 24, emphasising the importance of good general awareness when in possession of the ball.	1 Why is awareness important? **So that player knows where team-mates/opponents are and can make appropriate decisions as to what to do next.** 2 How is greater awareness achieved? **By occasionally looking up from the ball when in possession (more skilled performers can do this for longer)**
• Skill Practice 24	1 As for Skills Warm-up, only player not dribbling ball raises hand above head as dribbler approaches. Player dribbling calls out as soon as they observe this.	1 Time between hand being raised and dribbler calling out should be as short as possible.

Content/Organisation	Teaching Points
2 As for Skill Practice 1, only pairs dribble across diagonals of 10m square.	2 Players should be encouraged to dribble at a pace which enables them to maintain an awareness of the other pair (*ie.* look up) so that collisions are avoided.

A   1   D

          2

C   B

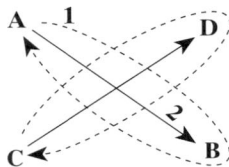

A dribbles ball around **B**, returns to starting position and passes to **B** who then dribbles around **A** etc. . . . Meanwhile **C** and **D** are performing the same practice.

• **Skill Practice 25**	1 In pairs, players dribble and pass within 20m square.	1 Encourage avoiding others with good awareness (looking around)
	2 Develop above so that players with ball dribble until teacher/coach blows whistle. Ball should then be stopped with the bottom of the foot and partner begins dribbling.	2 This practice may be developed so that non-dribblers take over any ball when whistle is blown.
• **Conditioned Game**	**'Through the Arches'** Players are in pairs within 20m square. Half of the pairs make arches around the square. The other pairs have a ball each and dribble around the area. The player dribbling passes through an arch to their partner. They receive the ball and dribble on to the next arch whereupon the exercise is repeated. How many passes can they make through the arches in 30 seconds. Change over.	Ensure the arches are well spaced out around the playing area. Players may only pass through the arches from close range (1m) – hence the need to dribble with the ball.
• **Conclude Session**	Reinforce intended learning outcome.	1 When dribbling with the ball what is it important to do? **Have a good awareness of the situation**
		2 How is this achieved? **By looking around as well as at the ball**

8–9 YEARS: SESSION 4

- **Intended learning outcome:** Consolidate and develop learning from sessions 1–3. Introduce players to basic game strategies of when to pass and when to dribble.

- **Equipment:** Ball between two, marker cones, braids.

	Content/Organisation	*Teaching Points*
Warm-up	1 Group is divided into two lines facing each other 10m apart. Players pair off opposite partner and number themselves 1 and 2. A ball (**o**) is placed midway between each pair. Players jog on spot. On call '1' (or '2') those players perform activities below: – a) run forward to ball and backwards to return. b) as above only instead of running around ball players place foot on top of ball and then return. c) Player runs out, passes ball to partner, runs around partner, partner passes ball back to be stopped in the middle and player returns to starting position.	1 Spread out lines as much as possible. **A B C D** **o o o o** **E F G H** Make sure players keep jogging on spot. For activities a and b, numbers '1' and '2' may be called out together.
Skills Warm-up/ Reinforcement	1 Ball between 2, 10m apart. **A** dribbles ball around partner, returns to starting position and passes ball to **B** whilst attempting to hit a marker placed 1m in front of **B**. **B** repeats.	1 The marker is introduced to promote accuracy of pass. Teach 'follow through to target' with striking foot. Players should be encouraged to pass with both feet.
Skill Development	1 Reinforce learning from previous 3 sessions.	1 During the skill practices, ask questions to check (and reinforce) previous skills learning.

	Content/Organisation	*Teaching Points*

- **Skill Practice 26**

1 Groups of 4 are split 2 × 2 facing each other 10m apart.

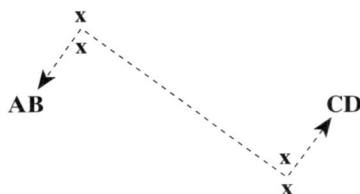

AB   **CD**

B dribbles ball through both gates and passes to **C. C** repeats and passes to **A** etc. . . .

1 Encourage close control, use of both feet and head up whilst dribbling.

Develop practice so groups of 4 race against one another. Each time they dribble through a gate they score. How many goals can they score in 30 seconds?

- **Skill Practice 27**

1 In 3's, **A** bounce feeds (ball is thrown underarm so that it bounces once on ground before reaching partner) to **B**, who controls ball on thigh and passes to **C. C** then feeds **A** who controls and passes to **B** etc. . . .

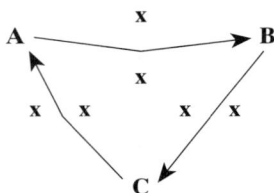

1 2m gates may be introduced to promote accuracy of passing.

Because the ball is arriving in one direction and being passed in another, players will need to be on the balls of their feet to adjust their body position to face ball whilst controlling and then passing.

Check eyes are on ball and head is steady whilst passing.

- **Conditioned Game**

Small-sided Games
Organisation as for Conditioned Game in 7–8 Years, Session 5. (page: 21)

Encourage the use of skills taught thus far in Sessions 1–4.

Note: dribbling skills (particularly when attempting to go around an opponent, are best employed in the opposition's half of the pitch).

Encourage players to be aware of their team-mates (and the opposition) by frequently looking around. Stress that passing the ball moves the ball down the pitch more quickly than dribbling.

	Content/Organisation	*Teaching Points*

• **Conclude Session**

Reinforce basic understanding of team strategies covered.

1 Which half of the pitch is it best/safest to dribble in? **Opponents *ie.* attacking half**

2 Why do you think this is so? **Ball is often lost whilst dribbling and this is dangerous in defensive half of pitch**

3 Which is the quicker way of getting the ball down the pitch, dribbling or passing? **Passing**

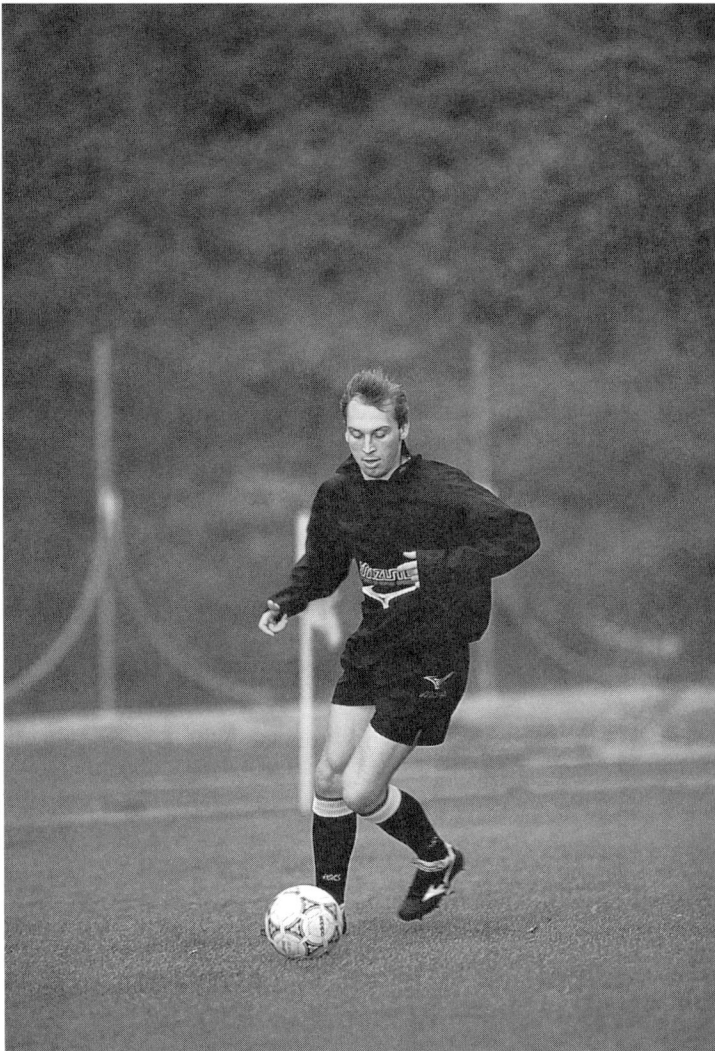

8–9 YEARS: SESSION 5

- **Intended learning outcome:** Develop heading skills, introducing the basics of attacking techniques.

- **Equipment:** Ball between two, marker cones, braids.

	Content/Organisation	Teaching Points
Warm-up	1 **'Mirrors'** One ball per pair, player with ball performs action with ball that partner must follow: – (i) Ball is bounced = partner jumps up and down (ii) Spin ball = partner turns around (iii) Hold ball above head = partner sits down (iv) Hold ball with one foot off the ground = partner hops	1 To introduce the warm-up, teacher calls out instructions for ball handler. After players have learnt the commands, they can work independently of the teacher. Change over roles every 30–45 seconds.
Skills Warm-up/ Reinforcement	1 In pairs, players make their way across a specified area. A ----→ B ----→ **B** (moving backwards) feeds ball to **A** (moving forwards) who heads back to **B**. When other side is reached, change over roles. 2 As above only player heading moves backwards and feeder forwards.	1 Players should remain about 2m apart and should not travel too quickly. Reinforce the heading techniques taught in 7–8 Years, Session 5 (page: 19). 2 This is a harder skill because the player is moving away rather than towards the ball when heading. Emphasise use of neck muscles.
Skill Development	1 Introduce basic techniques involved in attacking headers. If a headed demonstration is not possible, then throw the ball to show the flight it should take.	1 Attacking headers should be directed downwards towards the goal.

	Content/Organisation	*Teaching Points*
		Forehead should make contact with the top half of the ball. **Note:** this is more easily achieved if the ball is fed to the header along a flat trajectory.

- **Skill Practice 28**

1 In 3's, **A** feeds ball to **B** who tries to score in the 2m mini-goal. **C** retrieves ball. Players rotate around one place so that **C** feeds to **A** and **B** retrieves etc. . . . .

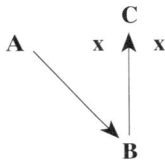

```
            C
  A    x  ↑  x
   ↘      ↑
      ↘   ↑
        ↘ ↑
          B
```

1 For accuracy, forehead must be directed towards target (goal) at impact.

How many goals can each group of 3 score in 30 seconds?

Safety: ensure player's mouth is closed whilst heading.

- **Skill Practice 29**

1 As above, only instead of standing directly in front of the goal, player heads from a slight angle.

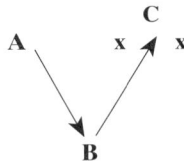

```
              C
  A     x   ↗  x
   ↘       ↗
     ↘   ↗
       ↘↗
        B
```

1 Again, the forehead should be directed towards the target at impact.

Widening the goals slightly will promote greater success.

- **Skill Practice 30**

'Throw-head-catch'
In 3's, **A** feeds ball to **B** who heads to **C**. Having caught the ball, **C** then feeds to **A** who heads to **B**. Teams make their way down the pitch until within range of goal into which they then attempt to head a goal.

How many goals can each team score in 2 minutes?

Encourage headers for goal to be directed downwards.

Note: this practice introduces a 'throw-head-catch' sequence which may be developed into a game between two sides.

- **Conditioned Game**

Develop game of '**Fetball**' (page: 25) using goals rather than benches. There is no need for goalkeepers.

If scoring is too easy/difficult then goal size may be increased/decreased accordingly.

- **Conclude Session**

Reinforce intended learning outcomes.

1 In what direction should an attacking header be directed? **Downwards**

Content/Organisation	*Teaching Points*
	2 How is this achieved? **Making contact with top half of ball**
	3 When should we use an attacking header? **When attempting to score**

8-9 YEARS: SESSION 6*

- **Intended learning outcome:** Employing a four station skills circuit, develop the skills covered thus far.

- **Equipment:** Ball between two, bean bags, benches, chalk, skittles, braids.

	Organisation/Content	*Teaching Points*
• Warm-up	See previous session.	
• Skills Warm-up/ Reinforcement	In pairs 8m apart, **A** rolls ball to either side of **B**. **B** moves into line with ball, picks it up and rolls it to the side of **A** etc....	Encourage players to get their body behind the rolling ball and to pull it into the chest once in their hands.
		Ball should be rolled approximately 2m to either side of player.
• Skill Development	Introduce the skill circuit *ie.* demonstrate the four activities comprising the circuit. Divide class into four groups and assign each one to an activity.	Make one clear teaching point for each activity.
		So that players remember what to do at the next activity when rotated, get them to watch the group in action on the activity they are moving to next.
• Skill Practice 31	**Activity 1:** *Heading* – in pairs, **A** performs sit-ups (legs bent, hands across chest) whilst **B** holds a ball so that as **A** comes up on each sit-up they can head the ball (which remains held). Change over after 10 attempts.	1 Use neck muscles to 'throw' forehead at ball.
		If player finds sit-ups difficult, allow their hands to be placed under the thighs. Also, **B** may anchor the feet of **A**.
	Activity 2: *Passing* – two benches are placed at right angles. Player passes against one bench, controls ball and passes against the other	2 Walls may be used instead of benches.
		Encourage control with foot nearest to bench about to be passed to.

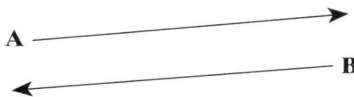

In the diagram between the warm-up rows:

A ————————→

←———————— B

If too congested, players to
work in pairs and take turns
after set number of passes.

If no walls/benches – use
players to return the ball.

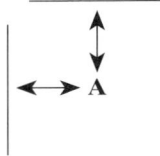

Activity 3: *Dribbling* – set
up a series of 2m gates made
from different coloured
beanbags. **A** dribbles through
which ever colour gate
(determined by colour of
beanbags) **B** signals. **B**
signals by holding up a
coloured card/beanbag each
time **A** passes through a
gate.

3 Encourage dribbler to look
for signal from **B** as soon as
possible having dribbled
through gate.

Encourage close control
(keeping ball close to foot)
and head up.

Activity 4: 'Skittle Ball'
Two teams of 4 ∨ 4. A skittle
is placed within a 2m
diameter chalked circle at
either end of the playing
area. Each team attempts to
knock their opponents skittle
over. Neither team is
permitted in either chalked
circle.

4 This game may be played
using football or netball (to
develop goalkeeping skills)
rules.

Players to decide on rules for
restarts.

Encourage correct skill
selection during game *ie.* to
dribble (in attack) and pass
(in defence).

• **Conclude Session**

Reinforce learning from
Activity 1.

1 Which muscles should we use
when heading?
Neck

2 Why do you think this is
important?
To achieve power

8–9 YEARS: SESSION 7

- **Intended learning outcome:** Develop goalkeeping catching skills at and above waist height – emphasising getting into position and good hand position.
- **Equipment:** Ball between two, marker cones, braids.

	Content/Organisation	*Teaching Points*
• **Warm-up**	In pairs players stand back-to-back jogging on spot. Number off '1' and '2'. When number is called out perform following activities: (i) 'circle' – run around partner (ii) 'jumps' – 5 star jumps (iii) 'tag' – have to tag partner (partner attempts to get away) (iv) 'tunnels' – pair have to go through each others legs.	If players are tiring from jogging on spot, then they should march (using bold actions). Intersperse activity with stretches.
• **Skills Warm-up/ Reinforcement**	1 In pairs 10m apart, **A** rolls ball to **B** along ground, runs around **B** and back to starting position. **B** rolls ball to **A** etc. . . .	1 Reinforce skill of getting behind ball and pulling it into chest once caught. Race – first pair to complete 5 rolls each.

• **Skill Development**	1 Introduce skills of catching ball at or above waist height emphasising the hand position when catching. **Note:** for catches above head height, hand position on ball can be demonstrated by turning back to class (briefly!) After all catches the ball should be pulled into the chest.	The basic goalkeeping stance should be adopted (page: 24) in preparation to catch. For catches at or below chest height, hands should be with thumbs pointing downwards and fingers well spread. For catches at head height or above, hands should be placed with thumbs up (so that a 'W' is formed between thumbs and forefingers).

Plate 5: The hands are positioned so that a 'W' is formed between thumbs and forefingers for this catch above head height.

• **Skill Practice 32**	1 In pairs, 5m apart. **A** throws ball at waist/chest height for **B** to save. **B** then throws ball for **A** to save. Each player is stood between a mini-goal 2m in width.	1 Look for palms pointing towards ball with fingers pointing downwards whilst catching. Develop practice so that ball is thrown to side of keeper and/or harder. Players should throw underarm and from a distance over which they can be accurate.
	2 Develop above so that players attempt to score into their partners goal. How many can they score in 5 attempts?	2 Ball is not allowed to go above head height.
• **Skill Practice 33**	1 As for Skill Practice 32 (i) only ball is fed to keeper at, and slightly above, head height.	1 Look for fingers spread, palms towards ball and the 'W' shape. Also, move feet to get into line with the ball.

	Content/Organisation	*Teaching Points*
• **Conditioned Game**	**'Handball'** As for Session 5 page: 51, only goals are scored by throwing the ball into the goal – teams to have goalkeepers.	A semi-circle around the goal area (2m radius) which only the keeper is allowed into should be marked out. Look for players getting into space when in possession of ball and good goal-keeping skills (remember to change the keepers over regularly).

Plate 6: Having been caught, the ball should be pulled into the chest.

• **Conclude Session**	Reinforce intended learning outcomes.	1 Who can show me the shape your hands should make when catching a ball below chest height? 2 Above head height? 3 What should you do once you have caught the ball? **Pull it into the chest so that it is safe from opponents and then look up to see where team-mates are**

8–9 YEARS: SESSION 8

- **Intended learning outcome:** Develop support play, emphasising the importance of dodging skills to get away from defenders.

- **Equipment:** Ball between two, marker cones, braids.

	Content/Organisation	Teaching Points
Warm-up	See previous session.	
Skills Warm-up/ Reinforcement	In groups of six, players stand in circle. **A** passes ball to **B** and follows it to where **B** is standing. **B** passes to another member of the circle and follows the pass etc....	Remind children of what they have to do by repeating instruction 'pass and follow'. Players should aim to take one touch to control and one to pass (two-touch).
Skill Development	Introduce the idea of getting away from (losing) the defender in order to support the player with the ball.	Encourage simple dodging skills to lose defender. To dodge effectively, player needs to be on balls of feet and adopt a slightly crouched running position.
Skill Practice 34	1 In pairs, on the command, **A** has to get away from **B**. Change over. Repeat several times. To be effective this practice needs to be done in a relatively restricted area (forcing players to dodge).	1 Encourage a good body position to dodge effectively. This is a tiring practice. Allow time for rest between 10 second periods of running. On command stop, players should stop ASAP – how far away have they got from their partner?
Skill Practice 35	Groups of 4 in 10m grid. Two stand on outsides of grid opposite one another. Other two (an attacker and defender) stand inside the the grid. The two outside have a ball each. The attacker attempts to 'lose' the defender and receive a pass from either of the outside players. Once received the ball is then returned.	This practice may be introduced using throwing and catching skills before progressing on to footballing skills of passing and control. Look out for dodging skills to lose defender. A tiring practice, regularly change over the two in the middle.

A

C D

B

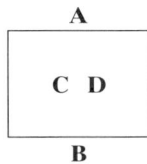

How many passes can an attacker receive in 20 seconds?

To prevent a series of short passes, attacker must return to centre of grid before receiving next pass.

Defender to follow attacker as closely as possible.

- **Conditioned Game**

As for Session 5, page: 51, only 5 ∨ 5 with goalkeepers.

Try and make any teaching points without interrupting the 'flow' of the game. If necessary, additional teaching can be delivered whilst teams are rotated round to face new opposition.

- **Conclude Session**

Reinforce intended learning outcomes.

1 What skill did we look at to help lose (*ie.* get away from) a defender?
   Dodging

2 What can we do to help improve our dodging skills?
   On balls of feet, slightly crouched position

8–9 YEARS: SESSION 9

- **Intended learning outcome:** Develop shooting skills, emphasising aiming for the corners of the goal.

- **Equipment:** Ball between two, marker cones/goals, skittles, braids.

	Content/Organisation	Teaching Points
• Warm-up	Players jog/brisk walk around 20m square. Each corner of square is given a different colour (*eg.* denoted by coloured beanbags). Players respond to following instructions: – a) Skip to yellow b) Side-skip to blue c) Run to red d) Circle arms up to green etc. . . .	Once players have reached the coloured corner (having continued in the same direction around outside of square to get there!) they continue jogging around square until next instruction is given.
• Skills Warm-up/ Reinforcement	1 Repeat Skill Practice 34. 2 As above, only in addition to giving instruction 'stop', periodically call out a number which players must get into groups of.	2 This adds a fun element – the children should be encouraged to get into the correctly sized groups ASAP and then return to their pairs to continue.
• Skill Development	Reinforce basic skills of shooting covered on, page: 28. Introduce the idea that (like a good pass) a good shot has the correct weight (power) and accuracy. Demonstrate the target areas (the goal corners) for shooting and set up the first practice.	Why are the corners of the goal the best place to shoot? **Hardest place for goalkeeper to save**
• Skill Practice 36	Repeat Skill Practice 15, only place a skittle in the corner of each goal to aim at.	How many times can they hit the skittle in 5 attempts?

	Content/Organisation	*Teaching Points*

• Skill Practice 37

As for Skill Practice 36 only instead of shooting from centre of goal, player is positioned slightly off centre and shoots across goal.

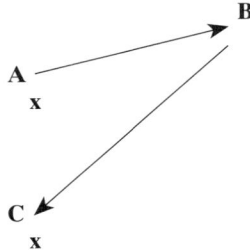

Encourage low shots by striking through middle of ball and getting knee over ball at impact. Also, head down and eyes on the ball.

Make sure the angle of shot is not too acute.

A skittle can be introduced at the far side of the goal to provide a target, with scoring as for previous practice.

Emphasise shooting across goal (*ie.* aiming at far post) rather than the near side (which is more easily protected by a keeper).

• Conditioned Game

'Pressure Shooting'
3 teams of 4 play in penalty sized area. One team retrieves balls and provides a feeder (F) and goalkeeper. Other 2 teams are in penalty area. One attacking the other defending. F feeds ball into attacking team who attempt to score. How many goals can they score in 1 minute? Change round teams.

Encourage players to shoot (towards the goal corners) at the first opportunity available.

Attacking players should follow the shot in for rebounds.

For this practice to work well, it is important that the ball retrieving team keeps the feeder well supplied with balls.

• Conclude Session

Reinforce intended learning outcomes.

Which areas of the goal should you aim for when shooting?
Corners
Why?
To prevent keeper from saving it

61

8–9 YEARS: SESSION 10

- **Intended learning outcome:** Develop players' understanding of how to support the player with the ball, focusing on basic triangular support.

- **Equipment:** Ball between two, marker cones, braids.

	Content/Organisation	Teaching Points
• **Warm-up**	See previous session.	
• **Skills Warm-up/ Reinforcement**	Groups of 4 around 10m grid.	Encourage an 'open body' position when receiving the ball (*ie.* player's body [**D**] faces mid-way between the on-coming ball [from **C**] and the direction of their pass [to **B**]).
	Pass ball around grid clockwise and anti-clockwise.	
• **Skill Development**	1 Introduce the best position to support a player with the ball. Demonstrate with group of 4 (3 attackers and 1 defender) working in 10m grid.	1 Introduce concept of support by encouraging players in support not to stand directly behind a defender (Skill Practice 38)
	2	2 Develop idea (Skill Practice 39) so that players support at corners of grid *eg.* **A** and **C** are in good supporting positions for **B** (right angled triangle) – if **B** passes to **A** then **C** must move to the free corner to support (and not be stood behind the defender).
	A, **B** and **C** are not allowed inside the grid – **D** attempts to gain the ball off them.	
• **Skill Practice 38**	1 Repeat Skill Practice 17.	1 Encourage players to move to the side of the grid not directly behind the player with the ball.
		Encourage defender to go to ball.

62

Content/Organisation	Teaching Points

• Skill Practice 39

Organisation as for Skill Practice 38, only players stand at corners (rather than sides) of grid. Each time ball is passed players should support player with the ball along nearest 2 sides of grid (*ie.* at right angles to them).

This practice may be introduced using throwing and catching skills so that players can concentrate more readily on the support aspect (rather than technical skills) of the practice.

How many times can the defender intercept the ball in 30 seconds?

How many passes can the attackers make in 30 seconds?

• Conditioned Game

Two teams of 4 v 4, play on 30 × 25m pitch.

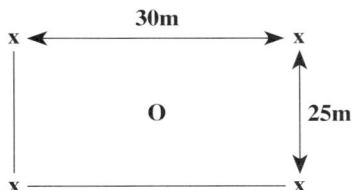

```
        30m
 x ←─────────────→ x
 |                 ↑
 |        O        | 25m
 |                 ↓
 x ─────────────── x
```

Team in possession attempts to knock down skittle in 2m diameter circle at centre of pitch. No players are allowed in the circle. When goal is scored (skittle toppled) defending team become attackers and re-start game from one of the marker cones at the corner of the pitch.

Players to bowl ball in underarm for throw-ins.

This game may be played using throwing and catching skills.

Encourage good support for the player in possession of the ball.

Briefly introduce concept of 'zone defence' *ie.* that defenders may defend space *ie.* stand around the circle rather than chase after the ball and attackers.

Note: game may be played with uneven sides eg. 5 v 3 or 6 v 2 to encourage attacking skills.

• Conclude Session

Reinforce intended learning outcomes.

Why shouldn't you support a player with the ball from behind a defender?
Because they can't pass it to you
What should you do if you are stood behind a defender?
Move to a position where the player with the ball can pass it to you

8–9 YEARS: SESSION 11*

- **Intended learning outcome:** Reinforce and develop learning covered in sessions 7–9, employing a four station skills circuit. Introduce the basics of the throw-in, emphasising releasing throw from back of the head.

- **Equipment:** Ball between two, marker cones, braids.

	Content/Organisation	Teaching Points
• **Warm-up**	**'Signal Response'** Players respond to the following visual signals in the manner indicated. Hand in air = jog clockwise around area Hand down = walk anti-clockwise Hand in air with thumb up = skip in clockwise direction Hand placed palm out in front = stop etc....	These signals may be added to and their meanings reversed for added complexity. Encourage players to respond ASAP to signals (the frequency of which should increase as familiarity with activity improves).
• **Skills Warm-up/ Reinforcement**	In pairs, 10m apart. **A** dribbles ball up to and through **B**'s legs before dribbling back to starting position. **A** then passes to **B** to repeat exercise.	Encourage use of both feet whilst dribbling and close control. Introduce race between pairs to complete set number of dribble and passes.
• **Skill Development**	1 Introduce the skill circuit ie. demonstrate the 4 activities and divide class equally around them.	1 Whilst the players are working on the four activities try and get around each one. Teaching points may then be made to the groups. Teaching points to the class may be made when moving groups onto the next activity.
• **Skill Practice 40**	**Activity 1:** In pairs, 6m apart. **A** throw-ins to **B**, runs around **B** and returns to starting position. **B** then throw-ins to **A** etc....	1 Hands behind ball in 'W' formation. Ball released from behind head. Both feet to remain on ground and bend knees. Encourage height on throw (*eg.* over a cross bar) to promote correct action.

Plate 7: A good throw-in position, with the ball about to be delivered from behind the head and both feet on the ground.

Content/Organisation	Teaching Points

Activity 2: In 4's, 10m apart.

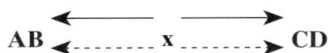

AB ◄------- x -------► CD

B dribbles to mid-point '**x**' and then passes to **C**, before joining back of **CD**. **C** then dribbles to '**x**' and passes to **A** etc. . . . .

2 Encourage accurate passing and close control whilst dribbling.

How many dribble/passes can they make in 30 seconds.

Activity 3: In 3's,

    5m   **5m**
A ◄---► B ◄---► C

A throws ball to **B** to catch, **B** throws ball back to **A** and turns whereupon **C** throws ball to **B** who returns it and turns to A etc. . . . .

Change player in middle after 10 catches.

3 **A** and **C** may throw ball in for **B** to catch at different heights *eg.* rolled along ground or above head height. This may be developed so that **B** does not know at what height the ball will be fed in.

Look for correct hand position on ball and pulling ball into chest.

Activity 4: Teams of 4 ∨ 4. Play on 30m square pitch. Each team defends two small goals (2m) placed 10m apart (no goalkeepers).

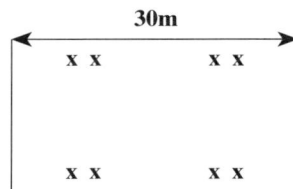

4 This game is designed to encourage players to look for width in attack.

Therefore encourage cross field passes which 'open up' the game and create space in front of the goal.

30m

x x   x x

x x   x x

(If indoors and space is insufficient, play '**Crab Football**' – as for Conditioned Game page: 27).

• **Conclude Session**

Reinforce intended learning outcomes.

1 What have we learnt about the throw-in today? **Ball must be released from behind head and both feet kept on ground during throw**

8–9 YEARS: SESSION 12

- **Intended learning outcome:** Conclude the year with a 5-a-side tournament. Reinforce techniques of throw-in during tournament.

- **Equipment:** 6 balls, marker cones, bibs/braids.

	Content/Organisation	Teaching Points
• **Warm-up**	See previous session.	
• **Skills Warm-up/ Reinforcement**	Organise teams of 5 for the tournament. Each group of 5 forms a circle (6m diameter). 'Pass (throw-in) and follow' activity. Player receiving throw-in catches ball and throws it to another player etc. . . .	With each throw-in, passer calls out the name of the player to whom they are throwing.
• **Skill Development**	Remind players of tournament format (page: 36).	When ball goes off sides of pitch, throw-ins to be taken.
• **Skill Practice 41**	As for Skills Practice 19.	Encourage players to call the names of their team-mates when passing ('put a name on the pass').
• **Conclude Session**	Draw attention to examples of fair play, good sportsmanship and helpfulness which occurred during the tournament.	The tournament represents the conclusion to a year's work – congratulate the children for all their hard work so that they look forward to next year's soccer programme.

For your notes

PART II TEACHING SOCCER TO 9–11 YEAR OLDS

Introduction The emphasis for 9–11 year olds should again be on activity and enjoyment with increased opportunities to employ newly learnt skills in game-like situations. By this age, children have the capacity to work in larger groups and co-operation and teamwork are skills which should be developed through practices and conditioned games involving the child in groups of up to five or six.

As the children's concentration span increases, so practices may run for longer before modifications need to be made. However, activities may need more differentiation as the diversity of ability levels in the class increases.

Increased spacial awareness at this age, opens up opportunities for teaching basic team strategies in attack and defence in addition to individual skills on and off the ball. Players may begin to develop strengths in either defensive or attacking skills and consequently perceive themselves as a defender or attacker. Despite this increased positional sense, all-round skills should still be encouraged.

Grouping the children according to ability will generally facilitate skills learning, but other forms of grouping should be utilised to develop broader learning objectives such as social interaction.

Having introduced the basic technical aspects of the game, these now need to be practised and mastered. The role of defensive players (opposition) in practices should gradually increase, thereby placing the children's skill levels under more pressure.

After 7–8 and 8–9 Years, the children's familiarity with the working routines in soccer sessions should improve and so they should be expected to organise themselves into practices more quickly. In addition, a greater level of fitness may be expected and consequently the intensity of practices should be increased whilst the need for rest between them decreases.

By devising rules and strategies, players should be expected to contribute more to formulating the precise structure of their games and this broadens the learning opportunities presented in a session.

The over-riding aim remains that **you and the children enjoy the soccer sessions**, as this helps create a positive learning environment essential for other objectives to be attained.

4   TWELVE SOCCER COACHING SESSIONS: 9–10 YEARS

9–10 YEARS: SESSION 1

- **Intended learning outcome:** Develop passing and control skills, focusing on employing one or two touches on the ball.

- **Equipment:** Ball between two, marker cones, braids.

	Content/Organisation	Teaching Points
• **Warm-up**	**'Football Statues'** Group stands in 20m square. Half the players have a ball and dribble in and amongst the remainder of the class who are spread within the area and jogging/marching on the spot. On command 'stop' all players stop ASAP. Dribblers then change over with joggers/marchers and activity continues.	Encourage dribblers to keep ball close to feet and keep head up. **Progression:** to promote good awareness, signal to stop should be a visual rather than verbal one.
• **Skills Warm-up/ Reinforcement**	Players jog in any direction within 20m square. 1 ball for every 3 players is placed in square and passed by two, and then one, touch amongst players as they jog.	Encourage players to call out the name of the person to whom they are passing. Passing should be over a short distance (no greater than 5m).
• **Skill Development**	Introduce concept of one and two-touch football. Demonstrate two-touch *ie.* control and pass. Demonstrate one touch *ie.* pass ball first time (no control).	Too many touches on the ball slows down play and gives the defending team more time to organise and win back the ball. One and two-touch football is particularly important in areas of the pitch which are congested with players (*eg.* in defending and attacking penalty areas and some congested midfield situations). It also promotes players' spacial awareness.
• **Skill Practice 42**	In pairs, using passing channels (Skill Practice 1) players stand 3–4m apart.	Encourage quality of work *ie.* a good first touch and accurate pass.

Content/Organisation	Teaching Points
Pass back and forth using two touches.	Practice may be developed so that players control with one foot and pass with other.
How many passes can they make in 30 seconds?	

• **Skill Practice 43**

1 As above, only players have one touch on the ball.	1 Develop practice by gradually building up to 3–4m passing.
Decrease the distance of pass to 1–2m.	
2 After a period of practice, see how many passes pairs can make in 30 seconds. Compare the scores made for two-touch and one- touch – which is higher?	2 Emphasise the importance of accurate and correctly weighted (how hard) passing. The ball should remain on the ground throughout the practice (foot through middle of ball).

• **Skill Practice 44**

In groups of 5, in 10m grid.

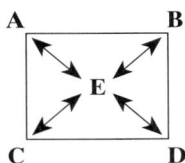

```
A            B
 ↖    ↑    ↗
   ↖  ↑  ↗
     E
   ↙  ↓  ↘
 ↙    ↓    ↘
C            D
```

A passes to **E**, who has two touches and passes to **B**. **B** has two touches and passes back to **E** and so on around the grid. After one circuit of the grid change the player in the middle.

Encourage **E**'s first touch to place the ball in such a position (approximately 1 foot in front) that it is easily passed to the next player.

E should attempt to remain in the centre of the grid during the practice.

Develop practice into races between teams.

• **Conditioned Game**

On 40 × 30m pitch, teams of 5 ∨ 5 (including goalkeepers) play two-touch game (*ie.* a player is only allowed to touch the ball twice in succession before another player must play it). A free-kick is awarded if a player takes more than two touches.

To develop confidence, start the game by allowing three touches.

Encourage accurate passing otherwise the game can deteriorate into a kick and rush affair.

Encourage players to look up before receiving the ball so that they are aware of passing options and defenders.

Finish the game by allowing full-touch (normal play) but encourage players that

73

	Content/Organisation	Teaching Points

Content/Organisation   Teaching Points

attempt to use two or one
touches, particularly when
space is restricted.

• **Conclude Session**   Reinforce intended learning   1 What do we mean by one
                              outcomes.   and two-touch football?
                                                              Player in possession touches
                                                              ball that many times

                                                            2 When should a player use
                                                              one or two-touch football?
                                                              When there isn't much space/
                                                              time *eg*. in the penalty area.
                                                              For fast breaks down the
                                                              pitch

9–10 YEARS: SESSION 2

- **Intended learning outcome:** Develop control skills, emphasising use of the chest as a controlling area.
- **Equipment:** Ball between two, marker cones and braids.

	Content/Organisation	*Teaching Points*
- **Warm-up**	See previous session.	
- **Skills Warm-up/ Reinforcement**	Pairs work in passing channels. **A** lob feeds (two handed under arm feed through the air) to **B**. **B** controls ball using any part of the foot. **B** picks up ball and lob feeds to **A** etc. . . .	Encourage close control by relaxing the controlling foot and cushioning the ball on impact.
	x 5m A ←——→ B x	If a player is competent at controlling with one part of the foot, challenge them to control using another part (*eg.* instep, outside, inside or bottom of foot).
- **Skill Development**	1 Introduce control on the chest.	1 The most difficult aspect of chest control is presenting the chest at the correct angle to the oncoming ball. The steeper the path of the approaching ball, the more the chest needs to be tilted upwards. As with all control, the ball should be cushioned and this is achieved by relaxing (and slightly withdrawing) the controlling area on impact. Arms should be held out to the side.
	2 If unable to demonstrate skill, show the target area for control (chest) and desired outcome of control (ball to land on ground within playing distance).	
- **Skill Practice 45**	In pairs 4–5m apart, **A** lob feeds to **B** who chest controls and passes back to **A**. After 5 attempts, **B** feeds to **A**.	This practice is made easier if the feed is on a relatively flat trajectory (so that the chest angle on control does not have to be altered too much).

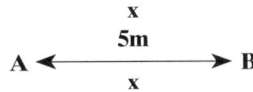

75

Plate 8: Both hands are placed under the ball in readiness for the lob feed, which must be as accurate as possible.

	Content/Organisation	*Teaching Points*
• **Skill Practice 46**	As above, but **A** feeds (by hand) the ball into **B** at ground, knee or chest height to control.	It is important that the controlling player is on the balls of their feet and ready to respond to the ball coming in at any height. The pass back to the feeder should also be executed accurately.

• **Skill Practice 47**

As for Skill Practice 46, only a control gate is placed 2m in front of **B**.

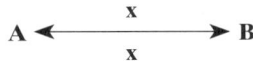

A ←———— x ————→ B
 ———— x ————

B attempts to control the ball without it rebounding beyond the control gate.

As players become more proficient the difficulty of the feed in should be increased. Thus the feeding player may progress to kicking the ball rather than rolling/throwing it.

• **Conditioned Game**

In groups of 8 on 20×15m pitch.

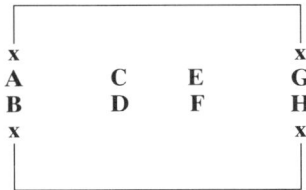

```
x                          x
A       C     E     G
B       D     F     H
x                          x
```

C and **D** play against **E** and **F**. Meanwhile **A** and **B** (and **G** and **H**) stand on the goal line and act as goalkeepers only they are not allowed to use their hands or come off the line. Change teams' roles over after 2 minutes.

This is a tiring game so it is important to change teams over regularly.

The goals should be wide enough (3–4m) to allow teams to score.

Finish game by playing $3 \vee 3$ (with 2 goalkeepers) on the same pitch.

• **Conclude Session**

Reinforce intended learning outcomes.

1 When controlling the ball what is it important to do with body part in contact with the ball?
Cushion the ball (take the pace off it)

2 How is this achieved?
By relaxing and withdrawing the controlling area on impact

9–10 YEARS: SESSION 3

- **Intended learning outcome:** Develop confidence on (with) the ball, introducing the skill of faking to kick, employing exaggerated movement.

- **Equipment:** Ball between two, marker cones, braids.

	Content/Organisation	Teaching Points
Warm-up	**'Teacher Says'** As for 'Simon Says' only teacher/coach holds ball up in air when instructions are to be followed (and down when not). Players stand well spread out in front of teacher. Instructions: – (to be carried out on spot) march, jog, run, jump, hop, touch ground, turn around, rotate arms etc. . . .	Players do not drop out if they make a mistake. However, challenge them by speeding up instructions. If ball is not held up whilst instruction is given, players continue with previous activity.
Skills Warm-up/ Reinforcement	1 Half of group in 20m square with ball each. Dribble in and around one another avoiding collisions. Remainder of group jog/ walks around square. On command, dribblers stop ball ASAP and change places with the joggers.	1 Encourage close control, good awareness of others and players to be on the balls of their feet ready to move in any direction.
	2 As above, only players attempt to kick each others footballs out of the square whilst protecting their own. Once player's ball is kicked out they join joggers – the last dribbler in the square wins.	2 To prevent each game from lasting too long set a time limit of 1 minute before changing dribblers over.
Skill Development	Introduce Skills Practice 48. Demonstrate the importance of exaggerating the fake/ movement to maximise its impact to deceive.	What is a fake (or dummy)? This is a move made by a player intended to deceive the opponent of their intentions.

| | *Content/Organisation* | *Teaching Points* |

- **Skill Practice 48**

In pairs, 5m apart. **A** passes to **B**, **B** controls ball and dribbles towards **A**. **B** fakes to kick ball to **A** and then dribbles around **A** and back to starting position. **B** passes to **A** etc....

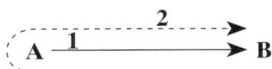

```
        2
   ┌---------→
 A ─1──────────→ B
   └- - - - - - -
```

To make the 'fake' effective player has to give the impression that the ball is going to be kicked. This is achieved by looking at the intended target and withdrawing the kicking leg in an exaggerated manner. To help with the fake, player should really imagine that they are going to kick the ball and then stop at the last instant.

- **Skill Practice 49**

In groups of eight, 4 pairs with ball each.

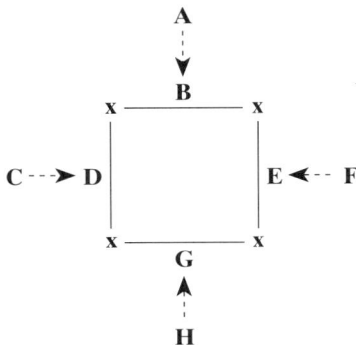

```
              A
              ┊
              ▼
              B
      X ─────────── X

 C ---▸ D         E ◂-- F

      X ─────────── X
              G
              ▲
              ┊
              H
```

Each pair (an attacker and defender) stands at side of 10m square. Attacker attempts to dribble ball around defender and into the square.

Encourage use of fake by attacker to make defender take evasive action before taking ball into square.

Attacker should start practice 8m back from square and should dribble (not kick) the ball into the square.

Defender is not allowed in square and should start practice mid-way between the attacker and square.

Change over roles after 3 attempts.

- **Conditioned Game**

Divide class into two teams within 20m square. Attacking team has a ball each and attempts to kick the ball against the other team (below knee height). If hit, player leaves square. How many players can the attacking team remove from the square in 1 minute?

Encourage use of the fake by attackers to deceive defenders into taking the wrong evasive action.

Note: good balance (promoted by flexed knees) facilitates the ability to fake.

Content/Organisation	Teaching Points

• **Conclude Session**

Reinforce intended learning outcomes.

1 What is a 'fake'?
A move intended to deceive an opponent

2 How can we make a fake effective?
Exaggerated movement and then change direction

9–10 YEARS: SESSION 4

- **Intended learning outcome:** Consolidate and develop learning from past 3 sessions in competitive situations.

- **Equipment:** Ball between two, marker cones, braids.

	Content/Organisation	Teaching Points
• **Warm-up**	See previous session.	
• **Skills Warm-up/ Reinforcement**	In 3's, A, B and C pass the ball around the triangle randomly. However, before each pass they must fake to pass to the free player.	Encourage exaggerated movement to 'sell' the fake to a defender. Players need to be on the balls of their feet and well balanced to execute the fake effectively. Players may demonstrate different ways of faking a pass – encourage this and show the group.
• **Skill Development**	1 Reinforce learning from previous three sessions. 2 Introduce competition (in the form of defenders) to the practices.	1 Whilst learning to master the basic skills, players will need to focus on performing the skill rather than the defender. As proficiency increases, so the player can begin to attend to the defender rather than the skill. To facilitate this transition use '**passive defending**' *ie.* defender attempts to disrupt, but not stop, the practice.
• **Skill Practice 50**	1 Ball between 4 in 10m square.	1 The speed at which the defender approaches the attacker (*ie.* pressure on the attacker) should be increased after each attempt.

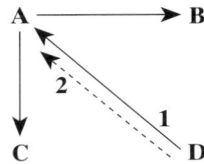

D passes (push pass along ground) to **A**. **D** then follows pass to defend against **A**. **A** must then pass to **B** or **C**. Repeat five times and change roles.

2 Develop practice so that attacker has to fake a pass (to the non-receiving player) before delivering the actual pass. Again build this up slowly so that the defender gradually increases pressure on attacker.

• **Skill Practice 51**

Organisation as for Skill Practice 50, only **D** lob or bounce feeds the ball to **A**.

Because control for **A** is now more difficult, **D** should not begin to approach **A** until after their first touch. As **A**'s competence increases the restriction on when **B** can approach should be made progressively less severe.

• **Skill Practice 52**

Ball between five in 10m square.

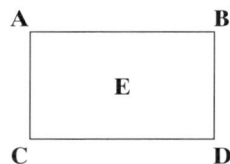

Players stand at 4 corners of square and pass ball to each other (randomly) playing two-touch football. Defender **E** attempts to intercept ball. After 5 successful passes a goal is scored and the defender should be changed. If defender intercepts a pass change with attacker making pass.

Begin practice with a passive defender *ie*. only trying at 50% to gain ball. As proficiency increases, defender should build to a 100% effort.

Remind players to concentrate on the skill (first touch and pass) and not the defender.

Encourage players to fake to pass before passing.

Defender should be encouraged to go to the ball and force a mistake (rather than waiting for one).

	Content/Organisation	*Teaching Points*

• Conditioned Game

Teams of 6 ∨ 6 play on 40 × 30m pitch. Normal soccer rules apply only each team nominates 4 attackers and 2 defenders. The 4 attackers from **Team A** must remain in one half of the pitch and play against the 2 defenders from **Team B**. The reverse occurs on the other half of the pitch. Thus each team has a 4 ∨ 2 attacking advantage.

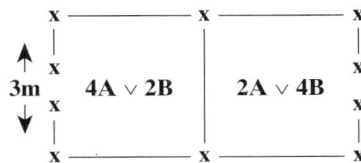

```
     x ———————— x ————————— x
     |                     |
  ↑  x                     x
 3m     4A ∨ 2B    2A ∨ 4B
     x                     x
  ↓  |                     |
     x ———————— x ————————— x
```

3m goals should be used and attackers and defenders changed over frequently.

This game is similar to netball in that players are restricted to zones of the pitch.

Defenders are allowed to pass to their attacking team-mates **unopposed** after a goal has been conceded or possession gained.

Encourage attackers to take advantage of their numerical superiority by using the full width and depth of their half (*ie.* spread out).

• Conclude Session

Reinforce basic team strategies covered in conditioned game.

1 Why do you think it is important to spread out when your team has possession?
To make it difficult for defenders to mark
To make space for the player with the ball
To make space for the ball to be played into

9–10 YEARS: SESSION 5*

- **Intended learning outcome:** Develop heading skills, introducing the basics of diving headers and emphasising 'throwing' the head through the ball.

- **Equipment:** One ball between two, marker cones, braids, mats/soft grass.

	Content/Organisation	Teaching Points
Warm-up	Arrange marker cones as below. Players brisk walk then jog around course. Complete course running, skipping, side-skipping and backwards running.	It may help to lead the players around the course for the first time. Changes in running style can be initiated: (i) on completion of each circuit. (ii) on teachers command. (iii) each time a marker is passed. Players should be evenly spread out around the course.
Skills Warm-up/ Reinforcement	In 4's, **B** lob feeds ball to **C** and jogs around behind **D**. **C** heads ball back to **A** and jogs behind **A**. **A** lob feeds ball to **D** etc. . . . Which team can complete 10 headers first?	Players to head through the middle of the ball returning it at approximately chest height. Encourage head to move at the ball (rather than being hit by it) by saying 'head through the ball'
Skill Development	Introduce Skill Practice 53. Explain that this is a progression towards learning diving headers.	The first practice is a safety one to ensure players are competent and confident to land safely after a diving header. Players should break fall by landing in the press-up position and lowering themselves to the ground.

Content/Organisation	Teaching Points

• Skill Practice 53

Players kneel on mat and fall forwards on to bent arms, landing in a press-up position.

Arms should be relaxed and out in front before falling forwards. Arms act as shock absorbers cushioning fall to the ground.

• Skill Practice 54

In 2's, **A** holds ball on palm of hand (so that it is teed up at head height) for **B** to head off. After 5 attempts change over.

Practice encourages use of neck muscles for heading and moving head at ball.

Keep eyes open and allow one step into the header.

Safety: thumb of palm should point away from player heading.

• Skill Practice 55

1 In 2's, **A** lob feeds ball to **B**. **B** is kneeling on mat and should have to fall forwards to make the header back to **A**. Change roles after 5 attempts.

2 In 3's, practice as above only heading player attempts to head past **C** into the goal.

1 The feed has to be accurate for this practice to work. Therefore feeding player should not stand too far from their partner (2m).

2 Players can progress from a kneeling to a crouched position before performing the diving header, providing their technique for landing after the header is safe.

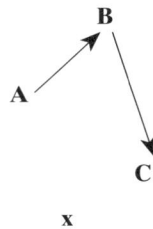

How many goals can each player score out of 5 attempts?

```
              B
            ↗  
        A ╱    ╲
               ╲
                ↓
                C
    x              x
```

• Conditioned Game

Teams of 2 ∨ 2 play in 8m square and defend goal the length of the end line.

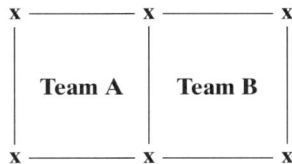

```
x ——— x ——— x
|      |      |
| Team A | Team B |
|      |      |
x ——— x ——— x
```

Team A starts game by player hand feeding ball for partner to head into the goal of **Team B**. **Team B** attempt to save the header (handling is allowed). If saved, the

Encourage partners to feed the ball in such a way as to allow the player heading to move into the header.

Players should not move with the ball once it has been caught.

Encourage attacking (downwards) headers as these are more difficult to save.

Change pairs around so that they face different opponents.

	Content/Organisation	*Teaching Points*

player making the save then feeds to partner to try and score into team **A**'s goal. Neither team may cross the half-way line. If a header is returned directly by a defending header (rather than being caught) a goal scored in these circumstances counts double.

Safety: diving headers should only be allowed if there is sufficient soft landing provision.

Rules for restarts to be determined by players.

• **Conclude Session**

Reinforce intended learning outcomes.

1 Which muscles should we use when heading?
Neck (and back for more advanced headers)

2 What do we mean by 'throwing' the head at the ball during the header?
Move head vigorously through the ball at impact

9–10 YEARS: SESSION 6*

- **Intended learning outcome:** Employing a four station skills circuit, develop skills covered in sessions 1–5. Introduce the basic block tackle, emphasising a strong crouched position and foot through the ball.

- **Equipment:** Ball between two, marker cones, braids, mats/soft area.

	Content/Organisation	*Teaching Points*
• **Warm-up**	See previous session.	
• **Skills Warm-up/ Reinforcement**	Class in pairs (**A** and **B**) within 20m square. **A**s have ball and attempt to keep **B**s from winning it by dribbling away from them. **B**s chase after **A**s, attempting to win the ball. Change roles after 1 minute.	If defender (**B**) wins ball inside minute, ball should be returned to attacker (**A**). How many times can the defender win the ball in 1 minute?
• **Skill Development**	Introduce the skill circuit. *ie.* demonstrate the 4 activities and divide the class equally around them.	Because block tackling is a new activity (and needs to be executed safely) you should spend the majority of your time with this group. **Safety:** shinpads to be worn if available.
• **Skill Practice 56**	**Activity 1:** *Block tackling* in 2's. **A** and **B** stand facing each other, hands on each others shoulders, with a ball at their feet. Simultaneously (on the count of 3) both players strike the ball. As confidence increases force behind tackle increases and players let go of shoulders.	1 Both players are performing the block tackle in this practice. Thus, they should be crouched at impact (for good balance and power), have their knee over the ball, use side of foot, and strike through the ball. **Safety:** gradually increase the force of tackle and match players for strength. The ball should not move during this practice.
	Activity 2: In 2's, in 8m square.	2 **A** and **B** are not allowed off their lines to pass through the goal. This practice may be made more difficult by introducing

87

```
x                    x

          x

A ─────────────────▶ B

          x

x                    x
```

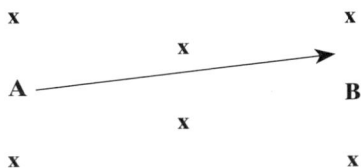

A passes ball through 2m goal, attempting to score into **B**'s goal. **B** attempts to stop ball and returns it through 2m goal, aiming for **A**'s goal.

restriction of two-touch or by reducing the size of the middle goal.

Ball should remain on the ground during practice.

Note: practice is easily adapted to involve 4 players by having two in each goal.

Activity 3: In 2's, **A** is in sit-up position and **B** stands in front with ball. As **A** reaches top of sit-up, **B** feeds ball to **A** to head back. Change roles after 10 attempts.

3 The timing and accuracy of the feed is vital for this practice to work. Thus, **B** should only feed the ball over a very short distance (1 foot).

A should use neck muscles to 'throw' head through ball.

Activity 4: 'Keep Ball' In groups of 5 within 15m square. 4 attackers attempt to keep ball away from one defender for 5 consecutive passes. If successful score a goal and change defender. If defender intercepts pass (or ball leaves square) then changes with attacker making pass or error.

4 Defender should be encouraged to chase the ball and force the mistake.

Restriction of two-touch may be introduced for most competent performers.

If skill level is low, this game works well as a throw/catch activity.

• **Conclude Session**

Reinforce intended learning outcomes.

1 What was the name of the tackle we looked at today? **Block tackle**

2 What can you tell me about how to perform the tackle? **Crouched, use side of foot, knee over ball, strike through ball**

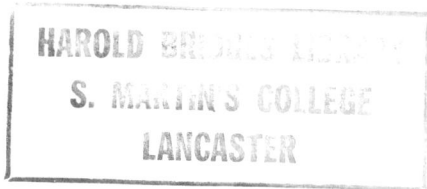

9–10 YEARS: SESSION 7

- **Intended learning outcome:** Develop goalkeeping skills, focusing on diving for the ball and pulling the ball into the chest with both hands.

- **Equipment:** Ball between two, marker cones, braids, mats/soft landing area.

	Content/Organisation	Teaching Points
• **Warm-up**	1 Group jog/brisk walk in single file around 20m square. Number off 1–4. When number is called out, sprint/run past everyone still jogging/walking and back to starting position.	1 Check players know their number (1's hands up etc. . . .) and that they remember who is in front of them. This is a tiring activity and should be interspersed with stretching.
	2 Develop so that when number is called they come into centre of square and perform 10 star jumps, sit-ups etc. . . . whilst rest continue jogging.	2 Plenty of praise is important to sustain quality work.
• **Skills Warm-up/ Reinforcement**	In 2's, 7–8m apart. x x A ←——————→ B x x Practice begins by **A** rolling ball along ground for **B** to catch and roll back etc. . . . Develop practice so that **A** attempts to roll ball (on ground) past **B**. **B** does likewise.	Ball should be pulled into chest after every catch. Keeper should attempt to get body behind ball. Keepers should be on the balls of their feet and ready to move in any direction. How many goals can they score in 5 attempts? Goal size and distance between keepers may be altered as appropriate.
• **Skill Development**	Introduce practices which progressively increase the confidence and competence of the player to make diving saves.	**Safety:** ensure there is a soft/ safe area onto which the keeper may dive *eg.* mats or lush/soft grass (hard muddy areas are not safe).

Not all players will enjoy the 'rough and tumble' of being a goalkeeper. Therefore, do not push players into going any further than they are confident/competent to.

Plate 9: From the seated position, the keeper falls to the ground and gathers the ball. Notice how the body is behind the ball.

Content/Organisation	Teaching Points

- **Skill Practice 57**

In pairs, **A** sits down with legs apart and straight. **B** (standing) feeds ball to the side of **A** (at **A**'s chest height). **A** gathers ball whilst rolling to the side and returns ball to **B**. Change roles after 5 attempts.

Keeper (**A**) should pull ball into chest and roll onto shoulder, whilst eyes are kept on the ball.

To ensure an accurate feed, **A** and **B** should be 2–3m apart.

Pace of feed may be increased as confidence grows.

- **Skill Practice 58**

Organisation as above only **A** squats (rather than sits). **B** rolls ball (along ground) to side of **A**. **A** falls behind ball whilst gathering ball into chest. Change roles after 5 attempts.

A > B

Keeper should get body **behind** ball rather than falling on top of it – this reduces risk of ball travelling under keeper.

Feeding player may kick the ball if sufficiently accurate.

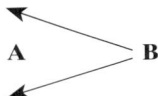

- **Skill Practice 59**

In pairs, **B** stands behind **A** who is kneeling. **B** rolls (by hand) the ball to either side of **A**. **A** (who must face away from **B**) must react quickly to fall on the ball as it passes.

B < A

The pace of the feed should gradually be increased, as **A**'s reactions improve. Too fast a feed and **A** won't have a chance!

For this practice, the keeper should fall **on top** of the ball and pull it into the chest.

- **Conditioned Game**

'Four Goals'
Teams of 6 ∨ 6 play on 40 × 30m pitch. Normal Soccer rules apply except each team defends **two** 3m goals and has two goalkeepers. Thus there are 4 keepers playing.

Four goals provide plenty of opportunity to shoot and make saves. Thus shooting should be encouraged.

Teams should look to 'switch' (move across pitch) play in order to open up scoring opportunities.

40m

x————————————x
| |
x   x
 (GK)   (GK)
x   x
| |
x   x
 (GK)   (GK)
x   x
| |
x————————————x

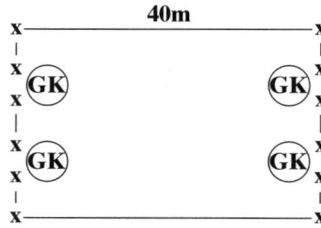

Regularly change over
keepers so that everyone has
a turn.

• **Conclude Session**

Reinforce intended learning
outcomes.

1 Why should a goalkeeper get
their body behind the ball if
possible?
**So that if a mistake occurs
the ball hits the body rather
than going into the goal**

2 After making a save, why
should the keeper pull the
ball into their chest?
**To prevent an attacker from
being able to kick it**

9–10 YEARS: SESSION 8

- **Intended learning outcome:** Develop defensive skills, focusing on the block tackle and 'jockeying' skills.

- **Equipment:** Ball between two, marker cones, braids.

	Content/Organisation	Teaching Points
• **Warm-up**	See previous session.	
• **Skills Warm-up/ Reinforcement**	In 3's, A ←----→ C ←----→ B C runs and block tackles with **A** (Skill Practice 56, page: 87). **C** then runs to **B** to repeat practice. As **C** runs towards **B**, **A** performs a throw-in to **B** who catches the ball and places it on the ground in readiness for the block tackle with **C**.	The force of the tackle should be dependent on the players' ability (group players of similar strength and ability). **C** should check forward momentum before making tackle *ie*. not run into it. **A** and **B** should take one step into the tackle. Check technique for throw-ins is correct. Change over roles after 10 tackles by **C**.
• **Skill Development**	Introduce the skill of 'jockeying' *ie*. holding up/ delaying player with the ball whilst backing off slowly. Demonstrate skills involved in Skill Practice 60.	To jockey effectively body position should be side on to the attacker and slightly crouched (monkey position). Player must be alert and on balls of feet shoulder width apart. Eyes focus on the ball, arms are held out slightly for balance and knees are bent.
• **Skill Practice 60**	In 2's 10m apart. xA ----→ A Bx ① ② **A** passes ball to **B** and jogs after it. **B** controls ball and dribbles towards **A**. **A** checks approach run 3m from **B** and begins to jockey. **B** continues	**A** should attempt to delay and not tackle **B**. However, if **B**'s control is poor and control is lost whilst dribbling, **A** should be close enough (1m) to toe the ball away. **A**'s approach run should be controlled and the jockey position assumed 3m from **B**.

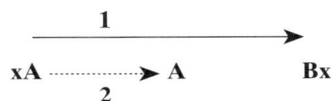

to dribble forwards whilst **A** jockeys to delay **B**'s progress. Once pair reach **A**'s starting marker practice is completed. Repeat 5 times and change over.

As **B** approaches, **A** should back off slowly retaining a distance of approximately 1m from **B**.

• **Skill Practice 61**

Organisation as above, only pair work in 8m square. **B** attempts to dribble to **A**'s starting line and stop ball on it, whilst **A** attempts to stop **B**.

x   x

A -------> <- - - - - - B

x   x

Change roles after each attempt.

This is a 1 ∨ 1 situation and is physically quite demanding, therefore 2 pairs may be rotated on and off the pitch allowing time for rest.

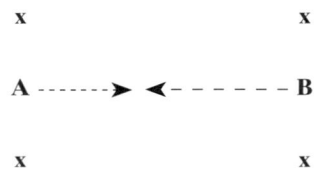

To make this practice easier for the attacker, the jockeying player may be restricted to jockeying only (*ie.* no tackles allowed).

Defender (**A**) must start practice on side opposite attacker (**B**).

• **Conditioned Game**

Repeat Conditioned Game for Session 4, page: 83

Concentrate on the work of the defenders during the game. Are they jockeying effectively? Because they are out-numbered, defenders should jockey rather than rush in to tackle.

Look for good technique on the block tackle.

• **Conclude Session**

Reinforce intended learning outcomes.

1 What is the purpose of jockeying?
   To delay the attacker and possibly force a mistake. Also to get support from defenders

2 Where should your eyes be looking whilst jockeying?
   At the ball

3 Why do defenders need to be crouched and on the balls of their feet to jockey?
   So that they can react quickly to anything the attacker does

9–10 YEARS: SESSION 9

- **Intended learning outcome:** Develop shooting skills – focusing on the volley, emphasising toe down, use of instep and head still at impact.

- **Equipment:** Ball between two, marker cones, braids.

	Content/Organisation	Teaching Points
• **Warm-up**	1 Players line up along one side of 20m square and cross it employing a series of different exercises *eg*. jog, side-steps, skipping, backwards run, jump and head (imaginary ball), touch ground, turn, sprint etc. . . .	1 Keep the group together and intersperse runs with stretches. Warm-up neck muscles in preparation for heading. (look left, right and up and down – repeat).
• **Skills Warm-up/ Reinforcement**	Ball between two, pair take turns to 'juggle' (keep ball off ground using any body part except hands and arms) ball in air. How many touches can they keep the ball in the air for? Can they beat their partner's score?	Players may start with the ball in their hands and bounce it on the ground to commence juggling (getting the ball off the ground with feet is quite a difficult skill). **Progression**: pairs may work together to juggle *eg*. heading back and forwards to each other.
• **Skill Development**	Introduce Skill Practice 62. **Safety**: demonstrate that accuracy (not power) is important at this stage. Contact point on ball should be through the middle and *not* underneath.	The volley involves striking the ball with the instep (or side of foot) whilst the ball is in the air. To be effective the player needs to be well balanced at impact – holding arms out facilitates this, as does a still head and eyes on the ball. The toe of the striking foot should be pointing downwards at impact.
• **Skill Practice 62**	In 2's, 5m apart. **A** throws ball up in front, allows it to bounce and then volleys to **B**. **B** controls (or catches) ball and volleys back to **A**.	Emphasise the importance of accuracy. Striking foot should follow through towards the intended target.

Repeat practice for weaker kicking foot.

Distance between players should be increased/decreased according to competence.

How many volleys out of 10 can their partner catch without having to move their feet?

Progression: ball is dropped and volleyed before it strikes the ground.

Plate 10: The volley technique – using the instep. Note how the toe of the foot points downwards at impact.

• **Skill Practice 63**

Organisation as above, only instead of self-feeding for volley, **A** lob feeds ball to **B** to volley back. Change roles after 5 attempts.

Player catching volley should place hands out to present a target for the volleying player to aim for.

	Content/Organisation	*Teaching Points*

- **Skill Practice 64**

In 3's,

A
x

C → B

x

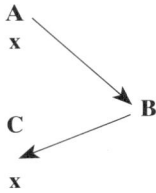

A lob feeds ball to **B** (from 5m) who attempts to volley the ball past keeper **C**.

Safety: if **B** is a powerful volleyer then **C** may retrieve the shot rather than attempt to save it.

The distance between players for this practice will depend on their power and ability.

For the practice shown, **B** should volley with the right foot. **A** should feed from the other side of the goal to practice **B**'s left footed volleys.

Encourage the volley to be kept low at impact by leaning forward, keeping the head over the ball and eyes on the ball.

How many goals can the volleyer score in 5 attempts?

Plate 11: Excellent balance after the volley has been executed. The head is still and down, whilst the arms held out to further improve balance.

	Content/Organisation	*Teaching Points*

- **Conditioned Game**

'Throw-Volley-Catch' Teams of 5 ∨ 5 play on 40 × 30m pitch with 3m goals at either end. Rules as for netball in open play except when ball is thrown to a team-mate it must then be volleyed before being caught and thrown again. Goals are scored with volleys (not throws).

Note: this is a difficult game and may require modifying *eg.* rules as for netball – *only* goals are scored with a volley.

The conditions of the game ensure plenty of opportunity to volley.

Encourage accuracy rather than power.

Change the goalkeepers over with outfield players regularly.

Safety: defenders may only intercept the ball **after** it has been volleyed and this is done by catching the ball.

- **Conclude Session**

Reinforce intended learning outcomes.

1 How can better balance be achieved when volleying?
   Keep head steady/still and arms out

2 Which part of the foot should be used to volley?
   Instep or side of foot

3 How can the volley be kept low?
   By leaning forward and over the ball with toe down at impact

9–10 YEARS SESSION 10

- **Intended learning outcome:** Develop players understanding of basic defending skills in a $1 \vee 1$ situation, emphasising getting low and sideways on.

- **Equipment:** Ball between two, marker cones, braids.

	Content/Organisation	*Teaching Points*
• **Warm-up**	See previous session.	
• **Skills Warm-up**	Ball between 4, groups work in 10m square. 3 attackers attempt to keep ball away from 1 defender. Defender changes places with attacker if intercepts their pass or forces a mistake. First pass can't be intercepted. **Progression:** attackers (or nominated individuals) play 2-touch.	Encourage good supporting angles for the player on the ball (right angled triangle). Defender to go to the ball. **Do not have the same player defending for extended periods of time**. Ball to be kept on the ground during practice. If attackers make 5 consecutive passes without defender intercepting, score a goal.
• **Skills Development**	Introduce players to the basic defensive skills in a $1 \vee 1$ situation. Demonstrate the sideways on and low stance to be adopted by the defending player.	The sideways on and low stance allows the defender to change direction quickly and react to the attacker.
• **Skill Practice 65**	In 4's, in 25×10m grid.	Your teaching should focus on the defender (**C**). Defender should: – move quickly to attacker and stop in a balanced low and sideways on stance. – prevent attacker from turning (*ie*. face **D**). If this can't be done, then should get close to prevent pass to **D**. – don't step backwards. – keep eyes on ball, not feet.

```
        10m
         A
10m      |1        10m
         |
x        B        x
         |
5m    2  |   5m
      :  |
x     C  | 3    x
         |
10m      ▼        10m
         D
```

Content/Organisation	Teaching Points

On attacker **B**'s call, **A** passes ball into **B**. Defender **C** allows **B** 5m start (use marker cones). As ball is passed to **B**, **C** quickly approaches **B**. **C** then defends against **B** who attempts to pass to **D**.

– be patient, don't rush in for the ball or foul.

• **Skill Practice 66**

Organisation as above, only defender **C** starts practice at side of grid.

As **A** passes to **B**, defender **C** should get across the pitch, get forward and get sideways on.

Note: **C**'s first move is across grid and this is to get between **B** and **D** thereby preventing an easy pass.

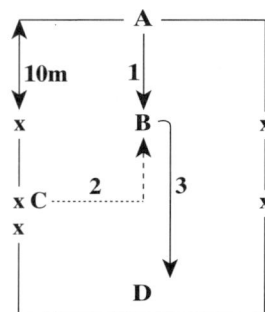

```
            A
        ┌───┐──────────┐
  10m   │  1│          │
  ↕     │   ↓          │
  x     │   B┐         x
        │   ↑│
      2 │   ↑│ 3
  xC····│···┘│
  x     │    ↓
        │    ↓
        └────┴─────────┘
             D
```

• **Skill Practice 67**

In 3's, grids as for Skill Practice 65 and 66.

Again, defender should get across, get forward and get sideways on.

C should not move until the ball has been passed by **A**.

Attacker **B** must dribble back to **A** within the grid.

How many times can the defender prevent the attacker getting past in 5 attempts?

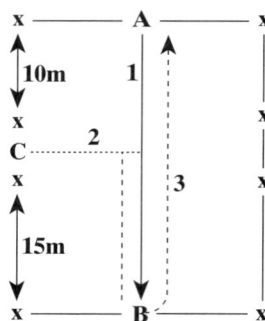

```
  x ──────── A ──────── x
  ↕          │↑
 10m        1│ ↑
  ↕          │ ↑
  x          │ x
        2    │ ↑
  C··········┘ ↑
  x          ↑│3 x
  ↕          ↑│
  ↕          ↑│
 15m        ↑│
  ↕          ↓↑
  x ──────── B◄──── x
```

On **B**'s call, **A** passes ball to **B**. Defender **C** attempts to prevent **B** from dribbling ball back to **A**.

• **Conditioned Game**

In groups of 5 in 20 × 15m square area, teams of 2 ∨ 2 play into one goal protected by a goalkeeper.

Players should decide rules for restarts.

Encourage players to defend in the manner practised.

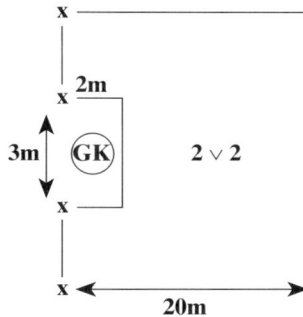

**Try and match groups of 5 so
that they are of similar
ability.**

Outfield players may not
enter 2m zone in front of
goal. The goalkeeper is
neutral and throws or kicks
the ball into the air to restart
play.

First pair to score 3 goals
wins and partner scoring
most goals changes places
with the keeper.

Introduce idea of 'man-to-
man' defence *ie.* players are
assigned a specific opponent
to mark every time the
opposition has the ball.
Periodically check if players
are marking their man. The
closer the attacker gets to the
goal the closer the man-to-
man marking must be.

• **Conclude Session**

Reinforce intended learning
outcomes.

1 What were the important
   defensive skills we looked at
   today?
   **Get to player quickly, get
   sideways on and get low**

2 Why is it important to get
   low?
   **To be able to react quickly
   to anything the attacker does
   (it improves balance)**

9–10 YEARS: SESSION 11

- **Intended learning outcome:** Reinforce and develop learning covered in sessions 7–10, employing a four station skills circuit.

- **Equipment:** Ball between two, marker cones, braids.

	Content/Organisation	Teaching Points
• **Warm-up**	1 Ball per pair, run around 20m square performing a series of activities. (i) throwing and catching to each other. (ii) roll ball back and forth (with hands). (iii) passing with feet. 2 Pair stand back-to-back and pass ball with both hands around themselves (change the direction). Pair pass ball over head and between legs.	1 It is important that pairs are well spread out around the square to allow room to perform skills. 2 Players should make their partner stretch to collect the ball.
• **Skills Warm-up/ Reinforcement**	In 2's, 6m apart. A ◄—x—————x—► B A and B stand behind a marker. A passes ball along ground attempting to hit B's marker. B controls ball and passes back attempting to hit A's marker. Score a goal each time marker is hit. Who can score 5 goals first?	Markers can be anything from beanbags to cones. Increase/decrease distance between passers to differentiate activity and/or restrict to one or two touches. Push pass technique is most effective for accurate passes over a short distance.
• **Skill Development**	Introduce the skill circuit *ie.* demonstrate the 4 activities and divide class equally around them.	Position activities so that interference between groups is minimised *eg.* goals should be positioned so that shots are directed away from other groups.
• **Skill Practice 68**	**Activity 1:** *Goalkeeping* – 2 balls between 3,	1 Shooting players should direct shot so that B can save it (*ie.* don't attempt to score). The intention being that B

x

A ——→ B ←—— C

x

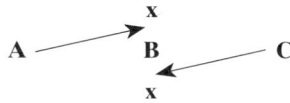

A and **C** have a ball each. **A** shoots for **B** to save. **B** saves and returns ball to **A**. **B** turns and defends goal from **C**, who shoots for **B** to save and then return ball.

If one ball goes astray, then shots should continue from other side until ball is retrieved.

Activity 2: *Pairs dribble and jockey* – within a 15m square. **A** dribbles within square whilst **B** jockeys. Change roles after 30 seconds.

Activity 3: *Throw-head-tennis.* In groups of 4, 2 ∨ 2.

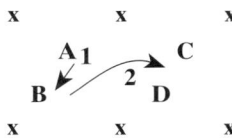

x   x   x

A 1 ——→ C
B ↙   2   D

x   x   x

A feeds ball for partner **B** to head over badminton height net. **C** or **D** catches ball and feeds for partner to head back. If ball hits the ground within a side's court boundaries they lose the point. Headers out of court lose point.

Activity 4: 3 ∨ 3 game played with normal Soccer rules with an additional 2 players acting as 'floaters'. These players always join the attacking side (the team with the ball), thus there is always 5 attackers

makes a rapid succession of saves.

If ball cannot be kicked in accurately then it can be thrown/rolled.

Keeper should aim to get body behind shots and pull ball into chest after each save.

2 Encourage close control by attacker and a low well balanced position for the jockeying player.

The jockeying player should not attempt to win the ball – merely delay **A**'s progress.

Players should remain 1–2m apart during practice.

3 Players are presented with the framework of a game here. They should create their own rules and scoring system to complete the game.

In order to direct the header upwards (and over the net) players will need to head through the lower/bottom half of the ball. This is made easier if the ball approaches the head (the feed) from a steeper trajectory.

4 The 'floaters' will take a little while to get used to their role and so shouldn't be changed over too quickly with other players.

Use braids/bibs to clearly distinguish floaters.

Content/Organisation	Teaching Points
versus 3 defenders. No goalkeepers, teams attempt to score in 2m mini-goals.	Team in possession should spread out across pitch to take advantage of additional players.

• **Conclude Session**

Reinforce intended learning outcomes.	1 If we want to head the ball upwards, which part of the ball should we head? **The bottom half and head through the ball**
	2 What rules/scoring systems did they come up with for 'throw-head-tennis'?

9–10 YEARS: SESSION 12

- **Intended learning outcome:** Conclude the year with a 'ladder' tournament.

- **Equipment:** Ball between two, marker cones, bibs/braids.

	Content/Organisation	Teaching Points
• **Warm-up**	See previous session.	
• **Skills Warm-up/ Reinforcement**	1 Put players into teams of four for the tournament. Teams divide into 2 ∨ 2, 10m apart,	1 Select teams so that ability level is spread evenly throughout the teams. Introduce one and two-touch restrictions. Ball should remain on the ground.
	AB ⟶ **CD** Pass and follow practice (see Skill Practice 7i).	
	2 How many passes can the teams make in 30 seconds?	2 Total all teams' scores. Can the group beat this score on next attempt?
• **Skill Development**	Introduce tournament format. Tournament is played on 4 mini pitches simultaneously.	All eight teams play at the same time. The team that wins the most matches in the allotted time wins the tournament.
• **Skill Practice 69**	**'Ladder Tournament'** The 'ladder' refers to the 4 pitches, which should be clearly numbered 1–4.	After each series of 5 minute games, ensure that teams know where to go. In the event of a drawn match flick a coin to decide the winner/loser.

	x x x
	     1 ⇌ 2
	 x x ⇃⇂ x
	     4 ⇌ 3
	 x x x
		The nature of the tournament means that teams will sometimes play each other more than once. Conditions such as two-touch may be introduced periodically.

	Number 1 is the 'top' pitch and number 4 the 'bottom'. Five minute games (no keepers and 2m goals) of 4 ∨ 4 start on each pitch. After 5 minutes stop the	Teams winning on pitch 1 and losing on pitch 4 may be changed over.

105

Content/Organisation	Teaching Points
games. The winning team moves up one pitch and the losing team down one. Teams that win on 1 and lose on 4 remain where they are.	Try to encourage and praise skills which have been learnt in the year.
Team winning most games during lesson wins tournament.	Resist the temptation to over-teach in this situation. This is a **fun** end to the year.

• **Conclude Session**

Emphasise the good points that came out in the tournament. Perhaps a good tackle, header or a team that tried particularly hard.	This is the conclusion to a year's work – congratulate the children for all their hard work so that they look forward to next year's programme.

5 TWELVE SOCCER COACHING SESSIONS: 10–11 YEARS

10–11 YEARS: SESSION 1

- **Intended learning outcome:** Develop passing skills, focusing on the 'wall pass' and emphasising the importance of weight of pass when passing into space.

- **Equipment:** Ball between two, marker cones, braids.

	Content/Organisation	Teaching Points
• **Warm-up**	1 Split players into 4 groups at corners of 20m grid. Jog/ brisk walk around grid remaining in groups until one lap is completed. Repeat exercise only jog 3 sides and sprint/run 1. Next, jog 2 and sprint 2, jog 1 side and sprint 3, sprint 4. One recovery lap walking.	1 Groups will inevitably spread out during sprints but should come back together whilst jogging.
	2 In between each lap perform stretches.	2 Stretches will allow recovery time between laps but shouldn't last longer than 30 seconds.
• **Skills Warm-up/ Reinforcement**	1 Organisation as for Skill Practice 71.	1 Encourage accurate, well weighted passes.
	2 Gradually decrease distance between sets of passers to 1m and introduce one-touch restriction.	2 This encourages a good feel for the ball and also good balance – players must be alert and on the balls of their feet.
	Introduce races for both practices.	
• **Skill Development**	Introduce the 'wall pass'. Demonstrate Skill Practice 70. Walk through it before building up to jogging speed.	The wall pass is an effective way of beating a defender, whereby the ball is passed in front, and received behind, the defender.
• **Skill Practice 70**	In groups of 7, 15m apart.	Players should concentrate on good technique whilst controlling, dribbling and passing.
		Player performing wall pass (**G**) should concentrate on passing into space for **C** to

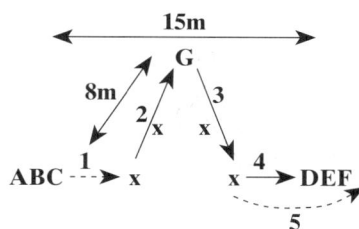

run onto ball. This is a complex skill and players should be given plenty of time to practise it.

It may be necessary to introduce this practice using throwing and catching to develop ability to pass into space.

C dribbles 5m to marker and passes to **G**. **C** accelerates run and collects pass from **G** at second marker 5m from **D**. **C** passes to **D**, joins queue behind **F** and practice is repeated etc. . . .

Change over roles so that all players practise the wall pass.

• **Skill Practice 71**

Organisation as above, only a defender is introduced and stands between the first and second markers.

Defenders role is a passive one *ie*. defender should act as an obstacle for the wall pass to be executed around.

Players should aim to speed the passing up as proficiency increases.

• **Conditioned game**

Game of 4 ∨ 4 played on 25m square pitch. A hoop is placed at each corner of the square. Team in possession attempts to score by stopping ball in one of the hoops.

Players to decide rules for restarts.

This is a good practice for introducing the concept of 'zone' defence *ie*. defenders mark space (in this instance a hoop) rather than an attacker.

Safety: (**i**) Defenders may not kick ball once it is in the hoop. (**ii**) Hoops should not be used on a surface on which they will slip (use chalked circles or skittles).

• **Conclude Session**

Reinforce intended learning outcomes.

1 What is the wall pass used for?
   Beating defenders.

2 What do you think the advantages are of a zone defence?
   Easier to be organised as a defence *eg*. less running about, everyone knows what they should be doing.

10–11 YEARS: SESSION 2

- **Intended learning outcome:** Develop passing and control skills, emphasising increased spacial awareness and communication between team-mates.

- **Equipment:** Ball between two, marker cones, braids.

	Content/Organisation	Teaching Points
• **Warm-up**	See previous session.	
• **Skills Warm-up/ Reinforcement**	In pairs, 10m apart. **A** juggles ball (see page: 95 Session 9 Skills Warm-up) whilst **B** jogs around **A** and back to starting position. **A** then passes to **B** who commences juggling as **A** runs around **B** etc. . . . Players may bounce ball on ground to commence juggling.	To start juggling (*ie.* get ball off ground) foot is placed on top of ball. Ball is then pulled back onto the same foot which is quickly positioned under the ball allowing the toes to lift the ball up. **Note:** practising juggling promotes a good 'feel' for the ball and consequently helps develop control.
• **Skill Development**	Introduce the concept of spacial awareness *ie.* the importance of being aware of what is happening around you (during a football game).	Do not worry if, whilst attempting to develop spacial awareness, there is a slight deterioration in skill level. This is because the player is attending to what is happening around them rather than performing the skill.
• **Skill Practice 72**	In pairs in passing channels (see page: 10). Each time player passes ball they should look over their shoulder before receiving the ball back.	Encourage players to use two touches. Players should look over alternate shoulders. Increase pace of passing as competence grows. **Note:** if ball is played too hard, then the practice breaks down.
• **Skill Practice 73**	Organisation as above, only 2 pairs work together. A ◄--► B ◄—► C ◄--► D (x over x between B and C)	Player receiving pass should check position of player behind them (defender) before the ball is passed in.

Content/Organisation	Teaching Points

A and D (defenders) stand 5m behind B and C respectively. If when B passes to C, D has moved to within 1m of C, C should pass back first-touch. If A has remained 5m back when B receives pass, B should control ball before returning it.

Change over roles frequently.

They should also be standing in the 'half turn' position (*ie.* their stance should allow them to see the defender and the ball).

Defender cannot change position once ball has been passed.

Develop practice so that passing player tells receiving player what to do *ie.* calls '**first time**' (1 touch) or '**hold**' (control then pass).

Practice may be simplified/introduced by only having one defender involved.

• **Conditioned Game**

Two 7-a-side games with goalkeepers are played on two halves of the same pitch.

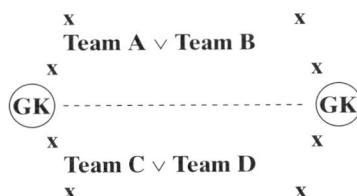

```
   x                    x
   Team A ∨ Team B
   x                    x
 (GK)------------------(GK)
   x                    x
   Team C ∨ Team D
   x                    x
```

Matches are not allowed to cross the mid-line of the pitch (a throw-in results if it does). **Teams A** and **C** shoot into the same goal (which bisects the mid-line) and **Teams B** and **D** shoot into the other goal.

This game limits teams to playing predominantly on the left or right hand side of the pitch. Change matches over so teams experience playing on both sides.

It also provides the keepers with plenty of action! (Don't forget to change keepers with outfield players)

Encourage players to look around before receiving or asking for a pass.

• **Conclude Session**

Reinforce intended learning outcomes.

1 Why should a player look around before receiving a pass? **To know where the opposition (and team-mates) are. To know what to do having received the ball**

2 What else can help a player know what is happening around them? **Team-mates talking to them and employing a 'half turn' when receiving the ball**

10–11 YEARS: SESSION 3

- **Intended learning outcome:** Develop confidence with the ball – introducing the skill of 'turning on the ball', emphasising the importance of a good first touch (control) and a sharp turn.

- **Equipment:** Ball between two, marker cones, braids.

	Content/Organisation	*Teaching Practice*
• **Warm-up**	1 In pairs, passing back and forth whilst running within 25m square area.	1 Pair remain within 5m of each other – avoid others.
	2 Label pair **A** and **B**. Whilst **A**s run around outside of square, **B**s dribble within square. **B**s can pass to any of the **A**s who must return the ball as quickly as possible. Stretch before changing over roles.	2 Encourage short and accurate passes which **A**s can return without having to stop running. Make sure **A**s are well **spread out** around square.
• **Skills Warm-up/ Reinforcement**	'Dribble and follow' In groups of 6, 3 ∨ 3 15m apart. **ABC** **DEF** **C** dribbles half way towards **D**, who jogs out and takes the ball of **C**, before dribbling on to **B**. **C** continues run (without ball) and joins queue behind **F**. **B** then dribbles half-way for **E** to take-over etc. . . .	Encourage a 'slick' change over in the middle. Dribbling player should present ball at side for partner to take-over. Players should not contact one another whilst taking-over the ball. Encourage close control and head looking up for awareness of partner. Race – first team to have everyone dribble 3 times?
• **Skill Development**	Introduce Skill Practice 74. Demonstrate progression from controlling and then turning (slower) to controlling and turning simultaneously (quicker).	If you don't feel competent to demonstrate the skill, then 'shadow' it *ie.* move through the skill without the ball. Turning on the ball is an important skill, especially in attacking areas of the pitch where it provides a sight of goal.

	Content/Organisation	Teaching Points

• Skill Practice 74

In 3's (**A** and **C** 10m apart),

A ———▶ B ⌣———▶ C

A passes ball to **B**. **B** controls ball, turns and passes to **C**. **C** passes to **B**, who controls ball, turns and passes to **A** etc. . . .

Change the middle player after 10 passes.

Encourage B to be alert (on balls of feet) and have a good first touch, enabling a sharp turn on the ball. **Note:** B should adopt a slightly side on stance and control the ball with the back foot (*ie.* the one furthest from the passing player).

To help with the turn, the first touch should place the ball slightly to the side (rather than directly under the player). This then provides room to turn. **Note:** controlling with the outside of the foot facilitates placing the ball to the side.

• Skill Practice 75

Organisation as above. **B** to control and turn with ball in one movement.

As player controls ball, body should be turning to face other way. This can be achieved by player controlling with inside or outside of foot.

It is important that the ball does not run too far away from the player during the turn.

• Skill Practice 76

In groups of 6, in 10m square.

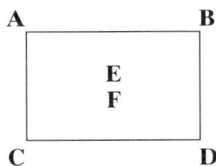

A   B
┌──────────────┐
│   E   │
│   F   │
└──────────────┘
C   D

A, **B**, **C** and **D** stand at corners of square. In square **E** is an attacker and **F** a defender. **E** starts with ball and passes to any of the corner players. They control and return ball to **E**, who turns on the ball and passes to any of the other corner players. They pass back to **E** who turns and passes again etc. . . .

The role of the defender should be passive to begin with *ie.* act as obstacle for **E** to turn around. As competence increases, defender may become more active.

E should not get too close to the passing player, remaining approximately in the centre of the square.

Ensure all players have a go at turning and practice using the inside and the outside of the foot to initiate the turn.

113

Content/Organisation	Teaching Points

• Conditioned Game

Teams of 6 ∨ 6 play on 40 × 30m pitch.

Organisation as for Conditioned Game, Session 4 (page: 83) only 3 attackers versus 2 defenders in each half and both sides have goalkeepers defending 3m goals.

Condition of play is that goals resulting from a player turning and shooting count double.

If player making a pass to a team-mate sees that that player can turn then should call '**turn**' to them.

Encourage team-mates to communicate to each other – this is a vital part of teamwork.

• Conclude Session

Reinforce intended learning outcomes.

1 What is required for a sharp turn on the ball?
A good first touch, balance and a good body position

2 Which part of the pitch is it most effective to turn in?
The opponents' half particularly in attacking positions

3 How can you help your team-mates on the pitch?
By communicating with them *eg*. tell player on the ball if there is a defender behind them ('man on'), or if no defender is present 'turn'

10–11 YEARS: SESSION 4*

- **Intended learning outcome:** Develop confidence on the ball, introducing the skill of shielding the ball and emphasising getting the body between the defender and the ball.

- **Equipment:** Ball between two, marker cones, braids.

	Content/Organisation	Teaching Points
• **Warm-up**	See previous session.	
• **Skills Warm-up/ Reinforcement**	Organisation as for Skills Warm-up Session 3 (page: 112). ABC ◄·········· x ··········► DEF **C** and **D** have a ball each and dribble towards one another. At the mid-point (**x**) they stop their ball and continue dribbling across with the other players ball. **B** and **E** take ball off dribbler and repeat practice etc....	Players should place their foot on top of the ball to stop it dead. Encourage a slick change-over – players should avoid colliding into each other by employing good awareness and dodging skills. Which team can complete the most change-overs in 30 seconds?
• **Skill Development**	Introduce Skill Practice 77. Demonstrate how, by positioning the body correctly between the ball and defender, the distance between the two may be maximised, making it difficult for the defender to get to the ball.	Good shielding technique prevents defenders from getting to the ball and allows an attacking player to hold up play whilst their team-mates get up in support.
• **Skill Practice 77**	In 3's, in 15 × 10m grid. **C** passes to **B**, who shields ball from **A** (passive defender). A Bo ◄————— C As shielding technique develops, defender should try harder to get the ball.	If player **B** stands with back towards **A** and both feet along dotted line then it is relatively easy for defender **A** to get to the ball (**o**). If **B** adopts a half turn (towards **A**) and widens stance along solid line then the distance between **A** and the ball is increased. On receiving **C**'s pass, **B** should control the ball with the outside of the foot furthest from **A**.

115

Content/Organisation	Teaching Points

Can the player on the ball shield it from the defender for 15 seconds?

Change over roles.

• **Skill Practice 78**

Organisation as above, only **B** makes a 5m diagonal run (from **B1–B2**) to receive the pass from **C**.

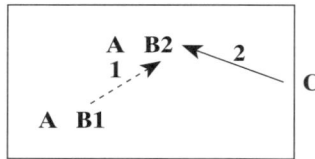

B's diagonal run helps to create the correct body position to shield the ball from **A**.

Ensure that the ball is controlled with the outside of the foot furthest from the defender and that the body is positioned as a barrier between defender and ball.

B controls ball and shields it from defender **A**, before returning pass to **C**. Return to starting position and repeat 5 times before changing roles.

• **Skill Practice 79**

All pairs in 20m square. Players without ball (defenders) attempt to kick other players' footballs (attackers) out of the square. Once ball leaves square, attacker becomes a defender. Who is the last attacker left in the square.

Encourage good shielding of the ball and change over attackers and defenders frequently.

• **Conditioned Game**

Two games of 7 ∨ 7 (with 4 goalkeepers) played on one pitch.

This is a good game if space is limited and it also increases the need for good spacial awareness.

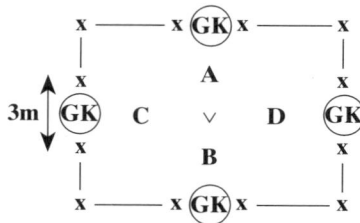

A fun game at the end of the session involves **Team A** combining with **Team C** to take on **B** and **D** (one or two balls may be used).

A play against **B** (up and down area) and **C** against **D** (across playing area). Normal soccer rules apply.

	Content/Organisation	Teaching Points
• **Conclude Session**	Reinforce intended learning outcomes.	1 What is the purpose of shielding the ball? **To prevent defender from getting to it and bringing team-mates into play**
		2 How is the ball shielded from an opponent? **Halt turn, widening stance and ball controlled with outside of furthest foot from defender**

Plate 12: Shielding the ball. Player has a wide stance and is controlling the ball with the outside of the foot furthermost from the defender. Also, in the half turn position, the shielding player can see both the defender and the ball.

10–11 YEARS: SESSION 5

- **Intended learning outcome:** Develop heading skills, introducing basics of defensive heading and emphasizing the importance of height and distance on the header.

- **Equipment:** Ball between two, marker cones, braids.

	Content/Organisation	Teaching Points
• **Warm-up**	1 Players run and dodge in 20m square.	1 To help change direction quickly, players should run in a slightly crouched position.
	2 When whistle blows, change direction of running 180 degrees.	2 Encourage quick responses to whistle.
	3 Get into pairs. **A**s to get away from **B**s and vice-versa (see Session 5 Warm-up page: 19).	3 Each time **A** and **B** change roles (every 5–10 seconds) perform stretches.
• **Skills Warm-up/ Reinforcement**	Half of group (the feeders) spread out around playing area. They have a ball each and stand still. The other half (headers) run around the feeders and receive lob feeds from them which they head back. How many headers can they make in 30 seconds? Change over roles.	Feeding players must wait until 'headers' are within 1m before feeding to them to head back. Headers must be aware of free feeders so that they do not all run to the same feeder. **Safety:** if 2 headers run to the same feeder, then they must take turns to head.
• **Skill Development**	Introduce Skill Practice 80. Demonstrate the path the ball should take either with a header or by feeding it.	The defensive header should be directed upwards and aim for maximum distance. This is achieved by heading through the bottom half of the ball, using the arms to pull the body into the header. Feet should be approximately shoulder width apart (one in front of the other) with knees bent, enabling legs to drive into header.

	Content/Organisation	Teaching Points
• **Skill Practice 80**	In pairs, 5m apart. **A** lob feeds to **B** who heads back to **A**. A piece of rope may be strung up (or a chalk line marked on a wall) for headers to aim over. After 5 headers change over roles and repeat.	Check header is using forehead to contact ball and that eyes are kept open for as long as possible. Maximum distance is achieved by timing the drive of the legs, back and neck muscles into the bottom half of the ball. **Safety:** do not repeat headers too often whilst skill is being learnt – poor technique can lead to a sore head!
• **Skill Practice 81**	In 3's (**A** and **C** 8m apart), **B** lob feeds to **A** who heads ball over **B** to **C**. **C** returns ball to **B**, whereupon **B** feeds ball for **C** to head to **A** etc. . . . Change roles after 5 headers.	Decrease/increase distance between players according to ability. More advanced performers may jump off ground whilst performing the header. Timing is the key here, the ball being met at the top of the jump.
• **Skill Practice 82**	In 6's (3 ∨ 3), 5m apart. **ABC**　　　**x**　　　**DEF** **C** lob feeds to **D** and runs behind **F**. **D** heads ball to **B** and runs behind **A**. **B** catches ball and feeds to **E** etc. . . .	To enable practice to flow, players should concentrate on making headers as accurate as possible. To achieve this the forehead should be directed towards the target at impact. A player may be positioned at **x** so that headers have to be directed over this player.
• **Conditioned Game**	Game of 3 ∨ 3 played on 25 × 20m pitch. Normal football rules only use 2m goals (no keepers) and two-touch. Finish game with full touch.	This should be a fast game with players linking up short passes. Encourage players to pass in front of the defender and look for a quick return pass behind the defender.
• **Conclude Session**	Reinforce intended learning outcomes.	1 What should you aim to do with a defensive header? **Aim for height, distance and away (wide) from the goal area**

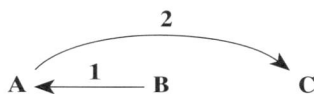

Content/Organisation	*Teaching Points*
	2 How can you achieve distance and height on your headers? **Use leg, back and neck muscles to launch into ball. Head through the bottom half of the ball**

10–11 YEARS: SESSION 6

- **Intended learning outcome:** Employing a four station skills circuit, develop skills covered in sessions 1–5. Teach game of 'Soccer Rounders' to introduce concept of team strategy.

- **Equipment:** Ball between two, marker cones, braids, benches, hoops.

	Content/Organisation	*Teaching Points*
• **Warm-up**	See previous session.	
• **Skills Warm-up/ Reinforcement**	Ball between two, pair take turns to juggle ball (see Skills Warm-up Session 9, page: 95). How many times can they keep the ball up using feet, thighs or heading only or combinations of these?	Players should bounce feed (drop ball on floor) to start juggling if unable to use feet. Players should set targets for themselves. Can they beat their previous best score? (in this way players are challenged at their own ability level)
• **Skill Development**	Introduce the skills circuit *ie.* demonstrate the 4 activities and divide the class equally around them.	'Soccer Rounders' – Allow time for players/teams to develop strategies for this game. Ask them to explain what they are.
• **Skill Practice 83**	**Activity 1:** Two benches are laid on sides 20m apart.	1 Look for players controlling and turning simultaneously. The inside or outside of the foot may be used. Good balance is essential and is promoted by players being on the balls of their feet during the control phase of the practice.

5m x   x

◄──► ◄------► ◄──►

x   x

Players pass against one bench from 5m out, control and turn on rebounded ball and dribble until 5m away from other bench. Pass against that bench and repeat practice.

If insufficient space/benches pairs should alternate performing ten turns and 10 sit-ups.

The ball should remain on the ground and this is achieved by kicking through the mid-line of the ball and getting the knee of the striking leg over the ball.

Note: players may be used instead of benches to return the ball!

Activity 2: Group of 8 players stand in a circle. 2 balls are passed randomly across the circle. Players should put a name on the pass (*ie.* call out the name of the intended recipient of the pass).

2 Players need to be alert to ensure they don't pass to the same player.

Players may be restricted to one or two touches.

Activity 3: In pairs, in 10m square, **A** and **B** attempt to stop ball on each others end line in a 1 ∨ 1 situation.

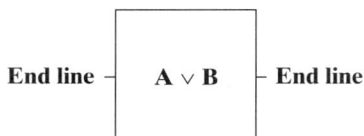

3 This is a tiring practice and pairs should alternate playing and resting with another pair.

Encourage shielding and jockeying skills.

End line ─| **A ∨ B** |─ End line

Activity 4: 'Soccer Rounders'
In groups of 4, **A** ('the batter') has 2 footballs (**oo**) to kick anywhere in front of two markers (**x**).

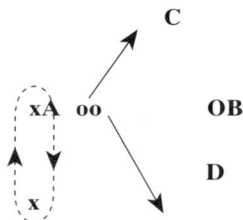

4 Encourage good technique when kicking the balls away. The instep (not toes) should be used if a powerful kick is required.

Look for tactical awareness. Where are the balls kicked? How do the fielders retrieve the balls? Do they work as a team?

                    C

xA oo   OB

                    D

Allow players time to develop their strategies before commencing the game.

B, C and **D** are fielders and must retrieve the balls (using their feet) and pass (or dribble) them to a hoop placed in front of **B**. Meanwhile, **A** runs between 2 markers (**x**) placed 10m apart, as many times as possible in the time it takes the fielders to get both balls in the hoop. Each player has a turn in bat. The player scoring the most runs wins.

Safety: balls should be kicked in a direction away from the other activities.

• **Conclude Session**

Reinforce intended learning outcomes.

Soccer Rounders
1 When you were in bat, what strategies (tactics) did you use?

2 When you were fielding, what strategies did you use?

10–11 YEARS: SESSION 7

- **Intended learning outcome:** Develop goalkeeping skills, focusing on the 'bowling' and 'overhead' throws employed by keepers to distribute the ball.

- **Equipment:** Ball between two, marker cones, braids.

	Content/Organisation	*Teaching Points*
• **Warm-up**	**'Traffic Lights'** Red = stop, Amber = walk Green = jog. Colours can either be called out or shown by holding up cards or objects.	Other colours (and activities) may be introduced once players are familiar with activity. To stretch mental faculties colours and commands may be reversed *ie.* red = jog and green = stop.
• **Skills Warm-up/ Reinforcement**	Organisation as for Skills Warm-up, page: 89. Ball may be delivered up to head height. Develop practice so that players feed the ball in more powerfully to each other.	Look for hand position on the ball when catching. Thumbs should be up for balls around head height and down for below. Ball to be pulled into chest after each save. **Tip:** tell the children to 'hide' the ball with their arms when pulling it into chest.
• **Skill Development**	Introduce the two basic throws employed by goalkeepers to distribute the ball.	A goalkeeper can quickly turn defence into attack with an accurate and well selected throw out. Both methods detailed below use one hand, the ball being held on the palm. **'Bowling' throw** – Ball is bowled underarm along the ground. Like an underarm throw, the throwing arm is kept straight and the ball held on the palm. Legs should be bent, allowing the ball to be released along the ground.

Note: players may need to use free hand to support side of ball before release.
Overhead throw – Similar in technique to an overarm cricket bowling action, the ball travels through the air and is delivered with a straight arm.

Plates 13 and 14: The overhead (13) and bowling (14) goalkeeper throwing techniques. Notice the ball is held with an upwards facing palm and delivered with a straight throwing arm for both methods. Both players are using their free arm to facilitate balance and have the opposite leg to their throwing arm forwards.

• **Skill Practice 84**

In pairs, 10m apart. **A** throws ball to **B**. **B** catches ball and throws it back to **A**.

◄--► A ◄——► B ◄--►

If throw and catch is completed successfully, both players take a step backwards. If unsuccessful (*ie*. throw fails to reach catcher), players take one step forwards. How far from each other can they get?

Introduce the 2 techniques one at a time and then practise as outlined.

A more side-on position should be adopted for the overhead throw. Also, look for a good shoulder extension of the throwing arm prior to delivery of the ball.

With both throws, the throwing arm/hand should follow through towards the intended target to ensure accuracy.

Plate 14: Bowling technique for goalkeeper throw-outs.

Content/Organisation	Teaching Points

• Skill Practice 85

Organisation as for Skill Practice 83(4). Player 'in bat' throws balls instead of kicking them. Fielders throw and/or place balls back in hoop.

Teams may need to be increased in size *eg.* 5 ∨ 5, so that games do not disrupt each other.

You may wish to introduce the rule that if the ball is caught, the batsman is out.

• Conditioned Game

Games of 5 ∨ 5 (including 2 goalkeepers), normal soccer rules. Play on 40 × 30m pitch with two 3m goals. Goalkeepers must throw the ball out (not kick it). Change the keepers over frequently so that everyone has a turn.

When the keeper has the ball, encourage an early throw to a team-mate if possible. Also team-mates should spread out so that the keeper may throw the ball wide.

Remember: if in doubt, a long throw is safer than a short one.

• Conclude Session

Reinforce intended learning outcomes.

1 What do you think the advantages are of the keeper throwing the ball out quickly?
Can turn a defensive situation into an attacking one without giving the opposition time to re-organise

2 What do you think the dangers of a quick throw out are?
If ball falls to the opposition, then own team's defence may not be organised/ready

10–11 YEARS: SESSION 8

- **Intended learning outcome:** Develop defensive skills, focusing on positional play when marking an attacker and emphasising goal-side.

- **Equipment:** Ball between two, marker cones, braids.

	Content/Organisation	*Teaching Points*
• **Warm-up**	See previous session.	
• **Skills Warm-up/ Reinforcement**	In pairs, 10m apart,	Restrictions of one or two-touch may be introduced to increase the difficulty of the practice.

A ◄————— x —————► B

A cone/marker is placed midway between **A** and **B**. **A** and **B** pass ball back and forwards, attempting to hit the cone/marker. Which player is the first to hit the target 5 times?

Change over partners and repeat practice.

Players should aim for accuracy (foot through to target) rather than power. Thus the 'push pass' (striking ball with inside of the foot) should be used.

- **Skill Development**

Introduce one positional aspect of marking an attacker.

Demonstrate Skill Practice 86, drawing attention to the position of the defender in relationship to the attacker, goal and ball.

Introduce the concept of goal-side marking (*ie.* defender is positioned between the goal and the attacker when marking that attacker).

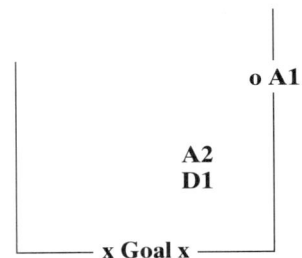

```
                          |
                          |
                          o A1
  |
  |
  |           A2
  |           D1
  |
  |____ x Goal x ____|
```

Attacker **A1** has the ball (**o**). The defender (**D1**) is marking **A2** and is goal-side.

	Content/Organisation	Teaching Points

• Skill Practice 86

In 4's, in 20 × 10m grid.

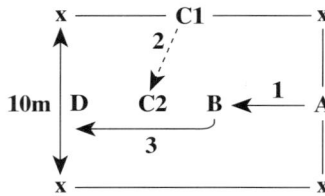

A has ball and passes to B. As ball is passed, defender C (stood at side of grid) runs from C1–C2 to get goal-side of B. After B receives pass, should attempt to pass ball to D.

If ball leaves grid, practice ends and should start again. Change roles after 5 attempts.

Teaching Points:

Player A should deliver the ball to B on their call.

Defender C should not attempt to play the ball until B has had a touch.

Once B has the ball, C should be between B and D.

How close should the defender stand to the attacker? If too close, ball is easily knocked passed defender. If too far away, attacker is under little pressure and can execute next skill unopposed. About arms length distance is effective.

• Skill Practice 87

Organisation as above, only C now starts the practice standing 2m behind B.

Note: B should perform a 3m diagonal approach run (B1–B2) before receiving the ball from A.

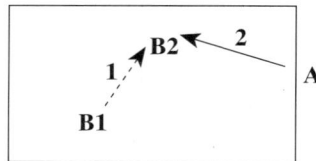

This opens up an angle and defender C must now get goal-side.

Teaching Points:

As the ball is fed in to B, C should be encouraged to get across and goal-side. C should be allowed to challenge for the ball as it is fed in.

Defender should be side-on knees bent (low), on balls of feet and eyes on the ball.

• Conditioned Game

In groups of 6, teams of 3 ∨ 3 play in 20m square.

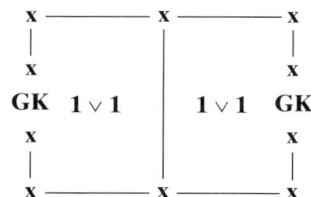

Teaching Points:

This is a tiring game and so players should be given an opportunity to rest whilst you reinforce the importance of goal-side marking.

Try and match defenders and attackers for ability.

Content/Organisation	*Teaching Points*
In each half, one attacker plays against one defender and a goalkeeper. Defender may play ball unopposed to attacking team-mate who attempts to beat the defender and score.	This game is easily adapted to a 2 ∨ 2 situation in either half of the pitch. Encourage forwards to turn sharply on the ball and get a shot in at goal.

• **Conclude Session**

Reinforce intended learning outcomes.	1 What positional aspect of defensive play did we look at today? **Goal-side marking** 2 Why do you think it is important to be goal-side of the attacker when marking? **To prevent them having a free run at goal if they receive the ball and to be nearer the goal if a pass is delivered over the top of the defence**

10–11 YEARS: SESSION 9

- **Intended learning outcome:** Develop passing skills, focusing on (crosses) pulling the ball back to the near post and emphasising head down and wrapping the foot around the ball at contact.

- **Equipment:** Ball between two, marker cones, braids.

	Content/Organisation	Teaching Points
Warm-up	Place beanbags randomly around playing area. Players to walk (then jog) in and around bags without touching them. Players to follow instructions: – (i) Run around 3 different coloured beanbags. (ii) Do 3 star jumps at 3 different red beanbags. (iii) Crab walk and touch three yellow bags. etc. . . .	**Safety:** emphasise that beanbags shouldn't be stood on.
Skills Warm-up/ Reinforcement	In pairs, each partner stands inside 1–2m square. A ⟷ B **A** lob feeds ball to **B**, who aims to control ball (using the thigh) within square. **B** then feeds to **A** to do likewise. Ball may be fed in by passing and/or at different heights. How many feeds can they control within the controlling square out of 10 attempts?	The size of the controlling square may be altered to accommodate the ability of the individual. Look for a good cushioning movement of the controlling area on impact. This is achieved by relaxing and slightly withdrawing the controlling area on impact. **Errors**: occur when player is tense and the controlling area is moved at the ball during impact, causing the ball to bounce away.
Skill Development	Introduce Skill Practice 88. Demonstrate the correct position and movement of the foot on the ball at	Crossing is an important technique for attacking football. Once players have spread out in attack it is important that wide players

130

impact, by placing foot next to ball.

(usually in more space) can cross the ball back towards the danger area in front of goal. Whilst power of kick is weak, players should aim to pull the ball back to the near post area when crossing.

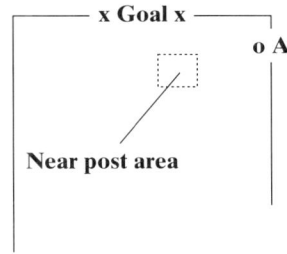

Near post area

• **Skill practice 88**

In pairs,

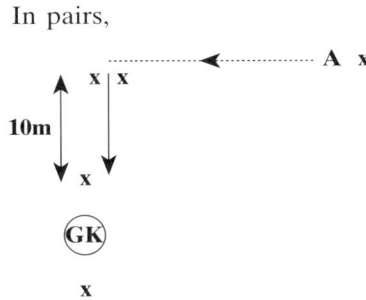

A runs with ball for 10m and crosses between 2 markers (**x**), aiming for the near post area. Goalkeeper (**GK**) saves ball and returns it to **A** at their starting position. Repeat 5 times and change over roles.

Players should cross with their preferred kicking foot.

Because players are striking the ball at right angles to the direction in which they are travelling, it is important that the kicking foot wraps around the ball during impact (*ie.* the kicking leg moves across the ball from inside to outside). The ball is contacted just below the middle.

Crossing player should look up at the near post area before delivering the ball there.

Important: players won't have enough power to cross the ball in from distance. Therefore, all crosses should be made over a 10m distance and no further. Also, crosses may be delivered along the ground or through the air.

• **Skill Practice 89**

In 3's, organisation as above.

Player **B** should time run so that they aren't standing still as the ball arrives.

Player **A** should look up before crossing to check the position of **B**.

Content/Organisation	Teaching Points

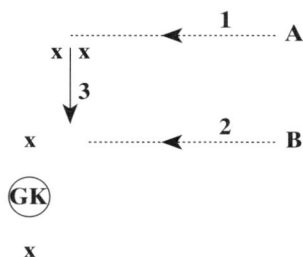

Player **B** starts run just after **A** in order to meet **A's** cross to the near post with a shot at goal. Keeper attempts to save shot.

Encourage player **B** to strike the ball first time (*ie.* do not attempt to control it).

Error: crossing player fails to wrap foot around ball and cross ends up behind the goal (emphasise striking the far side of the ball and head down).

• **Skill Practice 90**

In 6's, organisation as above only two goals are used.

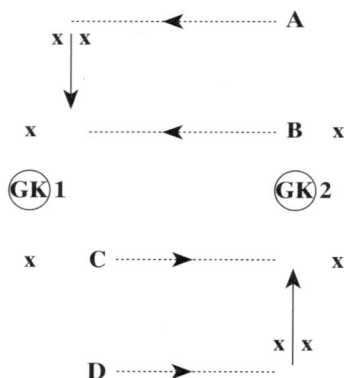

Keeper **GK1** throws ball to **D** after **A** and **B's** cross and strike. **D** then crosses for **C** to strike at goal. **GK2** throws ball to **A** who has returned to starting position etc. . . . .

Players must remember to return to their starting positions before commencing the next attack.

Note: the practice illustrated is intended for practising right footed crossing.

B and **C** should not run ahead of the player crossing the ball.

• **Conditioned Game**

Normal game of 5-a-side only two 2m crossing channels run along either side of pitch.

This game encourages players to collect the ball in wide positions and deliver a good quality cross.

Crossing channels should be no further than 10m out from goal. When team gains possession, the nearest players to the crossing channel should look to receive the ball.

```
x ——————————— x
|   crossing channel   |
x ——————————— x
|                      |
|                      |
x                      x
(GK)      5 ∨ 5      (GK)
x                      x
|                      |
|                      |
x ——————————— x
|   crossing channel   |
x ——————————— x
```

Note: only one attacker at a time is allowed in either crossing channel.

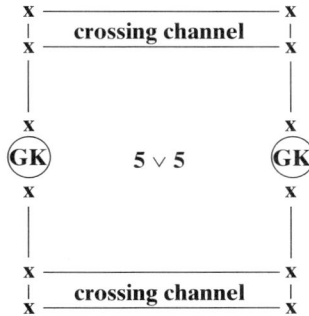

If attacker collects ball in crossing channel then they are allowed to run with the ball unopposed and cross.

• **Conclude Session**

Reinforce intended learning outcomes.

1 Who can show me where the near post area is?

2 What did you have to do to cross the ball into this area? **Keep head down and wrap foot around outside of ball**

10–11 YEARS: SESSION 10

- **Intended learning outcome:** Develop players' understanding of how to support the player with the ball, focusing on the skill of 'checking back'.

- **Equipment:** Ball between two, marker cones, braids.

	Content/Organisation	Teaching Points
• **Warm-up**	See previous session.	
• **Skills Warm-up/ Reinforcement**	In pairs, players take turns to juggle ball (see Skills Warm-up, page: 95). How many times can they play the ball before it touches the ground?	This activity is easily differentiated by allowing the ball to bounce on the floor to start and/or during juggling. **Error:** players may play the ball too firmly – reinforce the importance of good feel and touch for the ball.
• **Skill Development**	Introduce Skill Practice 91.	'Checking back' is a skill used by an attacking player to lose their marker.

B1 wants to receive the ball off team-mate **A**, but has to lose defender **C**. To do this **B** runs away from **A** and then checks back to position **B2**.

| • **Skill Practice 91** | In 2's, organisation as for Skill Development above, but without a defender.

A (with ball) and **B** stand facing each other 5m apart. **B** turns and runs a further 5m away from **A** before turning and checking back to receive a pass 5m from **A**. | Encourage a sharp check back by **B**. **B** should jog away from **A**, giving the impression of being disinterested in receiving the ball. On checking back, **B** should speed up running (thereby getting away from a marker) and call for the ball off **A**. |

	Content/Organisation	*Teaching Points*

Once **B** has received the pass, ball is returned to **A** for practice to begin again. Repeat 5 times and change roles.

• **Skill Practice 92**

Organisation as above, but when **B** checks back, run should be at an angle to **A**.

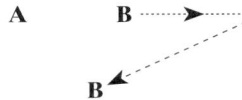

A   B ┈┈┈┈➤┈┈┈┈

          B ◄┈┈┈┈┈

The angled return run is intended to give **B** a clear sight of the ball and open up his vision of play (so that team-mates, ball and defenders can all be seen).

• **Skill Practice 93**

Organisation as above, but a defender is introduced into the practice (see Skill Development).

For this practice to work it is important that the defender attempts to mark **B** on the opposite side to **A** (imagining that **A** is facing the goal). Because the defender knows where the attacker is running to, his role should be a passive one.

• **Conditioned Game**

1 In 8's, using 10m square.

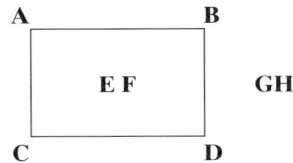

```
A                 B
 ┌───────────────┐
 │    E F    GH  │
 │               │
 └───────────────┘
C                 D
```

A, B, C, and **D** have a ball each and support the attacking player **E**. **E** attempts to get away from defender **F**, calls for ball off **A,B,C** or **D** and passes it back. Defender **F** attempts to stop **E** from successfully receiving and passing ball.

2 How many passes can **E** make in 30 seconds?

E and **F** change with **G** and **H** (who sit out and help retrieve wayward passes for 30 seconds).

1 This is a strenuous activity for the 2 players in the middle and they will need a rest after 30 seconds.

Encourage players to use the 'check back' to escape the defending player.

Players on outside of square should only pass the ball (along the ground) to the middle player when they call for it.

2 Players may be paired up (*eg.* **E** and **H**, **F** and **G**, **A** and **C**, **B** and **D**) and their individual scores combined to make a team total.

	Content/Organisation	*Teaching Points*
• **Conclude Session**	Reinforce intended learning outcomes.	1 What skills are required to make an effective 'check back'? **Pull defender away from where you want to receive ball and change direction quickly to receive pass**
		2 Why should the return run to the passer be at an angle? **To open up your field of vision so that you can see both team-mates, ball and defenders**

10–11 YEARS: SESSION 11

- **Intended learning outcome:** Reinforce and develop learning covered in sessions 7–10, employing a four station skills circuit.

- **Equipment:** Ball between two, marker cones, 4 skittles/cones, braids.

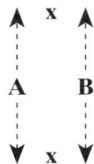

	Content/Organisation	*Teaching Points*
• **Warm-up**	In pairs, jog around outside of 20m square. Players to respond to the following instructions: – '1' = crawl through each others legs and continue jogging. '2' = pair perform 5 star jumps and continue jogging. '3' = pair sit down and then jog in opposite direction around square.	Introduce the activities one at a time. Encourage players to react to the number called out ASAP. Combinations of numbers may be called out, once players are familiar with activities.
• **Skills Warm-up/ Reinforcement**	In pairs, ↑ x ↑ ┊ ┊ A B ┊ ┊ ↓ x ↓ **A** has ball and attempts to dribble (with ball under control) to either of the two markers (placed 8m apart) before **B** gets there. **B** watches **A** carefully and tries to reach the marker first. Change roles after 1 minute.	**A** should try and deceive **B** by faking to go to one marker before dribbling to the other. This can be achieved by changing direction quickly and/or 'dropping the shoulder' to give the impression of moving in one direction and then moving in the other. **B** should not attempt to tackle **A**.
• **Skill Development**	Introduce the skill circuit *ie*. demonstrate the 4 activities and divide class equally around them.	Whilst players are participating in the skill circuit try not to stop them too frequently. Reinforce one clear teaching point as they are working.

• **Skill Practice 94**

Activity 1: In 3's,

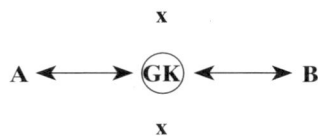

x

A ◄─────► (GK) ◄─────► B

x

A and B have a ball each. A rolls ball into goalkeeper (**GK**) to make a save. **GK** saves and throws ball back to **A**. **GK** turns and saves from **B** who has rolled ball in. **GK** returns ball and saves from **A** etc. . . .

Activity 2: 2 ∨ 1 in defensive channel (20 × 25m).

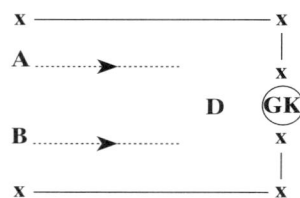

x ─────────── x
│
A ·········► x
x
D (GK)
B ·········► x
│
x ─────────── x

Attackers **A** and **B** attempt to beat defender **D** and score passed goalkeeper **GK**. Attacking pairs should line up behind **A** and **B**.

Activity 3: A throw-in practice, in 2's, 5–6m apart.

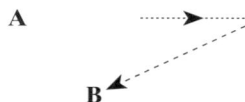

A ·········►
B ◄

A has ball, **B** turns and runs 5m from **A** before checking back to receive a throw-in from **A**. **B** controls ball and passes back to **A**. Repeat 5 times and change roles.

Activity 4: Game of 4 ∨ 4 played in 30m square.

1 Look for goalkeeper to get body behind approaching ball and to pull the ball into the chest with both hands after the save.

Progression: A and **B** feed the ball into **GK** at different heights and speed.

If ball goes astray during practice, **GK** should continue to save from one of the feeders whilst the other retrieves the ball.

2 **GK** is not allowed to come out from the goal and **D** must allow **A** and/or **B** to bring the ball 5m into the channel before challenging for it.

A and **B** should be encouraged to shoot if they get the opportunity and to pass if their partner is better placed to score.

D should go to the ball and attempt to prevent a clear shot at goal.

3 Emphasise that when **B** 'checks back' towards **A**, this run should be at an angle of approximately 45° to the run from **A**. In a game this angle opens up **B**'s field of vision, enabling him to see the ball, defenders and passing options.

A's throw should be delivered firmly and arrive at a comfortable height for **B** to control with feet (the throw should not bounce before reaching **B**).

4 Encourage the team in possession to attack the unprotected skittles *ie.* to be aware of where the defenders

```
          30m
   x ◄──────────► x
   │
   │   Ax          Bx
   │        4 ∨ 4
   │   Bx          Ax
   │
   x ─────────────── x
```

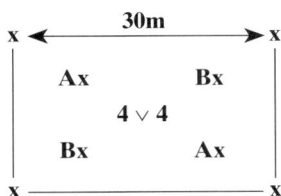

Four skittles (or cones) are placed at the corners of a 15m square at the centre of the playing area. Each team attempts to knock down their opponents two (A or B) skittles when in possession of the ball.

• **Conclude Session**

Reinforce intended learning outcomes.

are and play away from them.

If the ball leaves the playing area a throw-in should be taken.

Defenders will need to constantly adjust their position in order to defend both skittles and this requires **good communication** amongst the defending side.

1 Why is it important for defenders to talk to each other?
   So that they can defend as a team and help each other

2 What should they tell each other?
   Who to mark, where to cover and when to delay (jockey)

10–11 YEARS: SESSION 12

- **Intended learning outcome:** Conclude the year with a 'ladder' tournament.

- **Equipment:** Ball between two, marker cones, bibs/braids.

	Content/Organisation	Teaching Points
Warm-up	See previous session.	
Skills Warm-up/ Reinforcement	**'Copy Cats'** In pairs, **A** performs a trick with the ball which **B** attempts to copy *eg.* bounce ball on left thigh then right thigh or throw ball in air and catch behind back. Allow 3 attempts and change over roles.	Kicking and/or handling skills are allowed. Have a few tricks ready to help those short on ideas. Also, let those with good ideas demonstrate to the class.
Skill Development	Re-introduce 'ladder' tournament format (see Session 12, page: 105).	
Skill Practice 95	As for Skill Practice 69 but play 3 matches of 5 v 5 (with goalkeepers) on 3 pitches.	The first 5 minute games should be restricted to two-touch to encourage crisp passing and movement off the ball.
Conclude Session	Emphasise the good points that came out in the tournament.	Congratulate them on their progress and enthusiasm throughout the four years. Encourage the players to maintain an involvement in the game and draw their attention to any local clubs they might be able to join.

PART III   CONCLUSIONS

For your notes

6 ASSESSMENT GUIDELINES AND INTENDED LEARNING OUTCOMES

This chapter provides the teacher/coach with a check list of intended learning outcomes for each of the sessions which should form the basis for assessing each child's learning on the soccer programme.

It is recommended that:

- Assessment be a continuous process and used to facilitate future learning. It may prove helpful to record areas of weakness (or strength) which may be developed in subsequent sessions.
- Whenever possible assessment should be positive and based on what the child can realistically be expected to achieve. Try to focus on how far each child has progressed (what have they learnt?) during the sessions.
- A summative assessment at the end of each year be recorded to promote continuity and progression between years (this being especially important where groups change teacher/coach).
- The assessment procedure be as unobtrusive as possible. Thus, continuous informal assessment in the practical context should occur. Moreover, there is no need to record all that is assessed – only when there is evidence which is significant, such as evidence of achievement.
- Assessment addresses the three strands of 'planning', 'performing' and 'evaluating' running through National Curriculum Physical Education as this broadens the opportunities for each child to demonstrate learning.

The intended learning outcomes presented in the following tables, list the technical skills and some of the teaching/coaching points covered in each session. In addition, questions at the end of each session are presented throughout the text and these should help to assess the more cognitive skills involved in planning, evaluating and understanding performance.

Note: the intended learning outcomes listed are not intended to be exhaustive and other assessment criteria such as co-operation, honesty, confidence, leadership and so on, should form a part of the child's over-all assessment profile.

1. 7–8 Years: Intended Learning Outcomes

Session	Performance Skills
1	The 'push' pass – 'Monkey' position and inside of foot.
2	Controlling ball with the foot – relax and cushion.
3	Dribbling with the ball – ball close to feet.
4	Reinforce learning from sessions 1–3.
5	Heading – use of forehead and eyes open (mouth closed!).
6*	Skills Circuit. Team strategy – spread out in attack.
7	Goalkeeping – stance and pulling ball into chest.
8*	Movement after control and passing.
9	Shooting – use of the instep.

10	Introduce opposition – relax and concentrate on performing skill.
11	Skills circuit.
12	5-a-side tournament – round robin format.

2. 8–9 Years: Intended Learning Outcomes

Session	*Performance Skills*
1	Passing and control – importance of 'first touch'.
2	Control using the thigh – cushion ball on impact.
3	Dribbling – awareness of ball and playing situation, head up.
4	Reinforce learning from sessions 1–3. When to pass or dribble.
5	Attacking headers – contact top of ball to direct header downwards.
6*	Skills circuit. Use of neck muscles for heading.
7	Goalkeeping – catching techniques at, and above, waist height.
8	Develop support play – dodging skills to 'lose' defenders.
9	Shooting – aiming for the corners of the goal.
10	Supporting the player with the ball – basic triangular support.
11*	Skills circuit. Throw-ins – releasing ball from back of head.
12	5-a-side round robin tournament.

* Indoor sessions.

3. 9–10 Years: Intended Learning Outcomes

Session	*Performance Skills*
1	Passing and control – one and two-touch play.
2	Chest control – relax and withdraw chest on impact.
3	Confidence on the ball – faking to pass, using exaggerated movement.
4	Reinforce learning from sessions 1–3 in competitive situations.
5*	Diving headers – 'throw' head at ball.
6*	Skills circuit. Block tackle — strong body position and foot through ball.
7	Goalkeeping – diving for the ball, body behind ball.
8	Defensive techniques – the block tackle and 'jockeying'.
9	Shooting – the volley, toe down and use of instep or inside of foot.
10	Defensive techniques – 1 $\vee$ 1, get low and sideways on.
11	Skills circuit.
12	Ladder tournament

4. 10–11 Years: Intended Learning Outcomes

Session	*Performance Skills*
1	Passing – the 'wall' pass. Weight of pass.
2	Passing and control – increased spacial awareness and communication.
3	Confidence on the ball – turning, importance of first touch.
4*	Confidence on the ball – shielding ball, body between ball and defender.
5	Defensive heading – height, distance and away from goal.
6	Skills circuit. Awareness of team strategy.
7	Goalkeeping – 'bowling' and 'overhead' throws.
8	Defensive techniques – goal-side marking.
9	Passing – near-post crosses, foot around the ball.
10	Support play – 'checking back'.
11	Skills circuit. Develop communication.
12	Ladder tournament.

* Indoor sessions.